DECEPTIONS
OF THE
NEW
THEOLOGY

ISBN   0-923309-18-7

Deceptions
of the
New Theology

Table of Contents

This page intentionally left blank.

1

Roman Catholic Foundations of the New Theology

The term, *new theology*, was made prominent in the 1970s with the presentation by a number of popular preachers in the Seventh-day Adventist Church who taught that which to many appeared to be a beautiful, new, Christ-centered emphasis. These messages had an immediate appeal to many who had been trapped in legalism or who were insecure in their relationship with the Lord.

These people were attracted by the apparent Christ-centeredness of the message, and felt that they had an assurance now independent of any works that they must perform. Others saw it as an escape from the doctrinal emphasis that they had received in their Seventh-day Adventist upbringing. But the ultimate results have been seen in untold thousands leaving the Seventh-day Adventist Church. Tragically, many ministers and denominational workers have been numbered amongst this group. Many more thousands have accepted a Laodicean contentment in their carnal experience. Others have thought that their new liberation permits them to imbibe alcohol in moderation, to be free to use jewelry and colorful cosmetics, to use the Sabbath as a day for pleasure, and to deny the special ministry of Jesus Christ in the heavenly sanctuary.

The *new theology* message has been presented as a beautiful extension of Reformation theology, in stride with the teachings of Martin Luther and other Reformers. Few who hear this teaching understand the deceptive Roman Catholic heritage of its doctrine, designed to lull men and women into carnal security, and to bind them together for the great day of destruction at the conclusion of the millennium.

In 1978 Colin was speaking with Dr. Desmond Ford, the best known proponent of what is now termed the *new theology*. Dr. Ford had been inferring that the Adventist message was Roman Catholic. In response, Colin said, "You are not honest, Des, to call the Adventist message Roman Catholic." Rather graciously he responded, "Colin, perhaps you are right. I should not make such inferences." Colin responded, "Des, that is not what I'm talking about. You know, and I know, but hardly any of those who hear you know, that what you are teaching is unadulterated Augustinian Catholicism." The silence that followed indicated that he was not unaware of this fact. By the fourth century A.D., the Christian church was embroiled in theological turmoil. The centrality of Christ as man's Redeemer and His truth had been all but lost. Almost every wind of doctrine that could be presented was being preached. Church councils were assembled in a desperate and futile effort to determine orthodoxy. The church became the arbiter of faith in place of the Word of

God. Almost without fail, the decrees of church counsels took the church further and further away from the simple gospel of Jesus Christ.

Out of this theological milieu arose a man who was to be a giant in the formulation of theological dogma. Even today his shadow is cast across Christendom, and sadly his errors have been permitted to darken many corners of the Seventh-day Adventist Church.

Augustine was born in 354, in north Africa. While his mother was a Christian, his father was a Manichaean. Manichaeism was founded in the third century A.D. by Mani, as an offshoot of the ancient Persian religion of Zoroastrianism. This religious system was uncompromisingly dualistic. It had a special emphasis upon the dualism of light (good) and darkness (evil).[1]

All the pagan symbols were symbols of balance. The cross (the balancing of the horizontal and the vertical) is the most ancient and degraded of all pagan symbols. The Star of David, adopted as a symbol by the Jews, is an ancient pagan insignia incorporating the balancing of two triangles. The swastika of the Hindus and Buddhists is a balancing symbol as is the yin and the yang of the Chinese. It was this balance that led the pagans to have good and bad gods, male and female gods, and male and female priests. It was this concept which encouraged the belief that good and evil can reign together in the life. This satanic error had its origin in the Garden of Eden.

Augustine was nurtured in this pagan religion. When well into his twenties, Augustine went to Italy. There he studied under Ambrose in Milan, and subsequently accepted Christianity.

Augustine was unable to cast off all the pagan concepts which he had imbibed in his youth. His theological concepts thus were seriously influenced by this early mind-set. Yet his doctrinal perspectives were to dominate the training of church leaders until the time of Thomas Aquinas, who lived 700 years later. Many of the great theological errors of the Roman Catholic Church were either instigated by Augustine or developed as a result of subsequent theologians who attempted to formulate a consistent theology that would incorporate the Augustinian heresies.

Insightfully, Sister White understood this kind of situation:

> Men fall into error by starting with wrong premises and then bring everything to bear to prove the error true. In some cases the first principles have a measure of truth interwoven with the error; but it leads to no just action; and this is why men are mislead. They desire to reign and become a power, and, in the effort to justify their principles, they adopt the message of Satán (*Testimonies*, vol. 7, p. 181).

In a similar statement Sister White adds,

> They exalt themselves as men of superior judgment, and they have stood as representatives of God. These are false gods (*Testimonies to Ministers*, p. 364).

Roman Catholic theologians developed a very consistent and logical theology; but it was built upon wrong premises, premises that were inimical to the Word of God.

With his pagan mind-set, Augustine could not understand the issue of free choice. He saw God as absolute and in total control. A God who permitted man to have freedom of choice was incomprehensible to Augustine. Yet he discovered in the *Bible* the fact that some would be saved in the kingdom and some would be lost. To accommodate this truth into his theological concepts, Augustine introduced the doctrine of predestination.

The error of predestination was vigorously challenged in his lifetime. In response, Augustine argued that it is a miracle of the grace of God that any of us should be saved. Thus he suggested that we as erring humans were in no position to question the justice of God because He has preordained some to eternal salvation and others to eternal damnation.

This error of predestination logically led to the concept of once-saved-always-saved. God, being absolute and unchangeable, arbitrarily decided those who were preordained to salvation. These could never be lost. Those who were preordained to eternal destruction could never be saved. Naturally, this gave a presumptuous security to those who believed that they were preordained to be saved.

On the other hand, it also led to questions concerning the proclamation of the gospel. Why spread the message? Why evangelize? Why proselytize? If God's arbitrary will has predestined men to either salvation or damnation, what was the purpose of evangelism? The answer, which satisfied some, was simply because the Bible mandates it. Augustine's propositions upheld the view that the relationship of man to God was incidental to his salvation.

The dogma of once-saved-always-saved quickly incorporated the sin-and-live theology. No longer was victory over sin of any consequence to salvation. Vigorously Augustine argued that it would not be possible to gain victory over sin, even in the power of Christ. It will be noticed that each one of these unscriptural conclusions was a logical deduction from Augustine's false premise based upon his heathen belief that God does not permit man the power of free choice.

Augustine also popularized the concept of original sin, declaring that man was guilty not only of his own sin but, more importantly, he was guilty of the very sin of Adam. Sin was a state of being, not dependent upon man's desecration of the decalogue, though he did suggest that it was evidenced in acts of one's life. Initially he claimed that sex was the original sin. He had fathered an illegitimate child, and this exposed his long battle with sexual desire. This weakness left Augustine to search for a theological excuse for his sinful failures. Later he broadened the concept of original sin into other areas.

It was because of this concept that Augustine saw the man depicted in Romans 7:14–24 as a fully converted man. Unlike previous understandings which saw the man of Romans 7 as an earnest individual struggling and failing in human weakness, Augustine saw him as in a saved relationship with God. He ignored the plain testimony of Paul in relation to this passage.

> For we know that the law is spiritual: but I am carnal, sold under sin (Romans 7:14).

> For that which I do I allow not: for what I would, that do I not; but what I hate, that do I (Romans 7:15).

> Now then it is no more I that do it, but sin that dwelleth in me (Romans 7:17).
>
> For I know that in me (that is, in my flesh,) dwelleth no good thing: for to will is present with me; but how to perform that which is good I find not (Romans 7:18).
>
> O wretched man that I am! who shall deliver me from the body of this death (Romans 7:24)?

Augustine perceived the flesh and the spirit to be in cosmic tension. Never did he see the triumph of the spirit over the flesh. He did not understand the legalistic failures of this man nor the complete victory when he surrendered to the love and power of Jesus Christ.

> I thank God through Jesus Christ our Lord (Romans 7:25).
>
> There is therefore now no condemnation to them which are in Christ Jesus, who walk not after the flesh, but after the Spirit (Romans 8:1).

Indeed, in extant church literature, Augustine was the first to have proposed the concept that Romans 7:14–24 is describing a saved Christian. The torment of this man stands in striking contrast to the peace and assurance of God's children that is so frequently described in Scripture.

Augustine's view of original sin created a dilemma when he considered the incarnate Christ. If we were sinners just because we were born, then this would infer that Christ, too, was a sinner, for He, too, was born as we are. Of course, this was an intolerable thought. The Bible plainly described Christ as "that holy thing which was born of Mary" (Luke 1:35). Christ could never be described as sinful. Therefore Augustine was forced to conclude logically that Christ pos-

sessed an altogether different nature from man. Thus he postulated that Christ possessed the nature of unfallen man. In
this he ignored the plainest evidence of Scripture to the contrary.[2]

Since Christ was declared to have the human nature of an
unfallen man, this led the Catholic Church to espouse the
blasphemous doctrine of the Immaculate Conception, which
was fully incorporated into church dogma in the nineteenth
century. This doctrine declared that Mary was born of the
Holy Ghost so that she could have a son who possessed an
unfallen nature. Thus step by logical step, Augustine's false
theology led to the incorporation of numerous unscriptural
doctrines receiving acceptance by the Catholic Church.

But another dilemma arose. Christ was now far removed
from man. By placing Christ's human nature above our own,
it was difficult to accept Christ as our Mediator since, according to Augustine's view, He had not been tempted in the way
fallen mankind was tempted and tested. Neither could there
be any expectation that, even in His power, humans could
gain victory over sin. Surely, if man had a nature inferior to
His, as Augustine postulated, it would not be possible for
man to experience constant victory over sin such as Jesus had
while on earth. Augustine's inference was that Christ's sinless life was achieved because He held a great advantage over
us since He possessed an unfallen nature while we were
cursed with a fallen nature. Jesus ceased to be truly our Example.

Jesus thus was not in a position to succor those who are
tempted. The church was compelled to propose mediators

other than Jesus, men and women who most assuredly did experience and suffer (and yield to) like-temptations to us. Mary, the mother of Jesus, was proclaimed to be a mediator. Numerous saints were created by the church. These, too, became recognized as mediators. Upon the priests, who demonstrated themselves to be every bit as given to sin as their parishioners, was bestowed the role of mediator between God and man.

One step at a time, the church, in accepting these pagan concepts, was forced by logical deduction to add error to error in order to substantiate the false premises of Augustine. It soon became a dictum of the church that original sin separates man from eternal life. By the very act of being conceived, man was condemned to eternal torment.

These conclusions posed yet another question. How could the guilt of original sin be removed? The solution at which the church fathers arrived was by the act of baptism. The question then immediately arose as to the eternal fate of the unbaptized. The answer supplied was terrifying. They were condemned to eternal, burning hell. It is not difficult to imagine the impact of such a concept upon parents whose infants had died unbaptized. Infant mortality at the time was high. The anguish of sincere Christian parents of that generation, imagining that their children were tormented in eternal fire, does not bear contemplation.

The church quickly recognized that it had to supply a solution for this anxiety. Limbo was invented. Limbo certainly wasn't heaven, but neither was it hell. It was some intermediate place. But even this view did not placate the anguish of the parents. They would never see their little ones again. So the sacrament of infant baptism was introduced into Catholic dogma. There are many extant examples of priests sprinkling water over the abdomens of agonized mothers dying in childbirth, and then confidently declaring that both mother and child were assured of heaven.

Though some of Augustine's doctrines had been blunted by Aquinas and Abelard, two theologians of the Middle Ages, most of his theological concepts were still deeply rooted in Catholic theology at the time of the Reformation. It is important to recognize that Luther reacted more to the excesses of Rome, in the selling of indulgences by Tetzel in an attempt to raise money to complete the building of St. Peter's Basilica than he did to most of Rome's doctrinal positions. However, out of his study came one of the most beautiful discoveries of Scripture: "The just shall live by faith" (Habbakkuk 2:4; Romans 1:17).

Luther had been trained in the Augustinian monastery at Erfurt. He was an Augustinian monk. In his own writings he indicates that he had imbibed over and over again the works of Augustine before he had so much as set his eyes upon the Scriptures. Thus, while Luther was able to throw off almost all the post-Augustinian heresies, he retained almost all of the Augustinian errors. For example, Luther believed in predestination. He believed in once-saved-always-saved. He believed in the unfallen nature of Jesus Christ. He did not believe it was possible for Christians to constantly obey the law of God. He accepted infant baptism.

Thus, in the Reformed Protestant movement, Catholicism still had much influence. Indeed, many of these doctrines became more pervasive in the Protestant movement than they did in Catholicism itself. Some may ask why the Lutheran Church, generally speaking, does not accept predestination today. The answer is simple. After the death of Luther, Melanchthon led the Lutheran Church away from predestination. However, John Calvin, the Swiss Reformer, influenced the Dutch Reform Church and John Knox influenced the Presbyterian Church of Scotland to accept predestination.

Today the doctrine of predestination can be found not only in those churches but also in many of the Fundamental Evangelical churches, including the Baptist Church. It is this brand of theology that is knocking so vigorously at the door of the Seventh-day Adventist Church today. Tragically, many thousands of ministers and laypeople have opened the door wide to accept this insidious Roman Catholic invasion.

That which has been designated as the *new theology*, in fact, incorporates significant facets of ancient heresy. Today, many Seventh-day Adventists do not stand true to the clear principles of truth that God has enshrined in His Word. Many have either accepted varying degrees of Augustinian Catholicism or are confused by, or are unaware of, these dangerous heresies. The Augustinian influence is most clearly seen in the *new theology* on issues of the human nature of Christ and of sanctified Christian living. Only a daily Spirit-filled investigation of the Word of God will lead God's people away from the deadly errors of Augustine.

Endnotes

[1] All major pagan religions such as Hinduism, Tsaoism, Buddhism, Shintoism, and Zoroastrianism are predicated upon the concept of balancing numerous polar opposites, such as hot and cold; light and darkness; male and female; truth and error; young and old; good and evil; height and depth; far and near. The Chinese developed over 200 of these polar opposites.

[2] See chapter 5.

2

Historical Roots of the New Theology in the Seventh-day Adventist Church[1]

Many Seventh-day Adventists believe that the *new theology* is a phenomenon of the 1970s. But students of Adventist history have discovered that it has its origins in the earliest days of the Seventh-day Adventist Church. Soon after 1844, various fanaticisms and deviant viewpoints were expressed. Only the miracle of God could have led the handful of believers through the terrible disruptions of the 1840s and 1850s. Of those experiencing the disappointment of 1844, only a few were prepared to sincerely study in order to discover the mistakes that had been made by William Miller in the interpretation of the 2300-day prophecy of Daniel 8. Most returned to the sterility of their former churches. Some even renounced Christianity completely. Others formed the Advent Christian Church, a small body of Christians that continues to survive. It espouses Sunday sacredness, and has no major evangelistic thrust.

To those who studied the truths of the sanctuary message, it became clear that the cleansing of the sanctuary referred not to the destruction of the earth by fire, but to the commencement of Christ's Second Apartment ministry in the heavenly sanctuary.

Soon the small group of believers who correctly interpreted the 2300-day prophecy were bound together in their understanding that death was a sleep. They accepted the revelation of the Sabbath truth and the relationship of the law of God to the gospel.

Later they accepted revealed truth relevant to health and education. Yet, there were schisms. As early as the 1850s, the church, now known as the Church of God (Seventh Day), severed its connection with God's people largely on the issue of the prophetic gift of Ellen White. It, too, persists today as a small church. Fanaticism also entered, and a movement, very akin to the holy flesh movement of Indiana at the turn of the century, arose at this time.

There was further contention at the time of the organization of the Seventh-day Adventist Church in 1863. But wonderfully, in spite of all these issues, God brought His people together. Yet there were differences. The discussions on the divinity of Jesus Christ led to strong and heated expressions of opinion. The disagreement upon which law was referred to in the book of Galatians occupied much theological debate. The issue of whether the Ottoman Empire or the Papacy constituted the king of the north, was strongly contended. The issue of whether Daniel 8:11 referred to Roman paganism or Roman papalism was divisive. Even such trivial controversy as to whether the ten divisions of Europe included the Huns or the Alamani became an issue. But, in spite of these often heated differences, the Lord established a strong church, united upon the pillars and Fundamentals of the Seventh-day Adventist faith.

Yet unity was not without constant challenge from within. The *new theology* has its counterpart in the defection of one of the most able speakers and leaders of the early years of the Seventh-day Adventist Church, Dudley M. Canright. Much beloved by Elder and Mrs. White, he nevertheless wavered back and forth on his commitment to the message. By the 1880s, he had completely defected, never again to walk in the pathway of light. He became a most vigorous opponent of the Seventh-day Adventist Church. He repeatedly wrote against the sanctuary message and espoused a number of Augustinian principles in his theology. Even today his books against the Seventh-day Adventist truth are found widely distributed in seminary libraries across America and in other parts of the world.

By the turn of the century others were to challenge the unity of the faith. Prominent amongst these was Albian F. Ballinger. Ballinger had been a missionary to Great Britain, but by 1905, upon his return to the United States, he was strongly denying the sanctuary message and presenting a gospel built upon justification alone. He unquestionably was a forerunner of the heresy that so seriously disrupts the Seventh-day Adventist Church today.

A contemporary of Ballinger, Louis R. Conradi, became one of the most influential early proponents of the *new theology* in the Seventh-day Adventist Church. Conradi, as a young German living in the United States, accepted the Adventist faith in the 1870s. However, evidence indicates that he lost confidence in the Spirit of Prophecy over Ellen White's support of the messages of Waggoner and Jones, at the 1888 Minneapolis Conference. Thereafter, he was a constant critic of the Spirit of Prophecy and, though he assumed wide leadership responsibilities in the church, never did he fully support the truths held by our church.

For a time, Conradi was a missionary to the great German communities in the Ukraine region of Russia. Later he was appointed the president of the European Division where, almost single-handedly, he stifled the messages of the Spirit of Prophecy. He refused to have the Spirit of Prophecy manuscripts translated into German, and, probably more than any single individual, has been responsible for the indifferent and negative attitudes of many European Seventh-day Adventists to the Spirit of Prophecy. He did not believe in the sanctuary message. He did not believe in victory over sin. He believed in a *justification alone* theology.

It was Conradi who led many of the European church members into combatant service in the First World War, and, as such, precipitated the breakaway of the Reformed Seventh-day Adventist Church. As his influence became more questionable in Europe, he was called to the General Conference as a field secretary in the 1920s, but there his theological perspectives became so obvious that, under the leadership of the late General Conference president, Elder William Spicer, he was removed from the General Conference. And in 1932, at the age of 76, he separated himself from the Seventh-day Adventist Church, and became a minister for the Seventh Day Baptists.

During this time, however, Conradi had traveled widely. He had sought to influence many of the outstanding leaders to join him in his apostasy. On one occasion, the late Elder Roy Allan Anderson, onetime secretary of the General Conference Ministerial Association, told Colin that while he was an evangelist in England in the 1930s, Conradi had sought to enlist him to his apostasy. In the 1920s, Conradi had successfully influenced another Australian, Pastor William W. Fletcher. Fletcher was then chairman of the Southern Asia Division.

Upon returning to Australia, Fletcher became the chairman of the Bible Department at the Australasian Missionary College (now Avondale College). Here he began to teach a *new theology* very little different from that which was taught by Dr. Desmond Ford, four and five decades later. Alarmed, the then president of the Australasian Inter-Union Conference, Pastor Charles H. Watson, sent Pastor Fletcher to the General Conference, where for a couple of weeks he dialogued with a group of 16 or 17 leaders, including the General Conference president, W. A. Spicer. This proved to be of no benefit, and Pastor Fletcher was separated from denominational employment.

It is of deep significance that, according to a firsthand report by Dr. Athol Piper, Pastor Fletcher's desk drawers were full of Plymouth Brethren literature. Dr. Piper is the son of the late Pastor Albert H. Piper, who had the difficult responsibility of taking over, on a temporary basis, the Religion Department at the Australasian Missionary College when Pastor Fletcher was dismissed. The Plymouth Brethren Church teaches much in common with the *new theology*.

A few years ago, Colin had the opportunity to read W. W. Fletcher's book, written after his apostasy, entitled *The Reason for My Faith*. The striking parallel between his theology and that of Desmond Ford could not be ignored. In 1976 Russell spent time with Pastor Arthur Knight who had typed Pastor Fletcher's defense of his views almost 50 years earlier. Pastor Knight shared material with Russell which amply confirmed the fact that Pastor Fletcher had accepted many of the Augustinian errors.

As might be expected, the influence of W. W. Fletcher did not stop with his defection. His influence was to be witnessed again in the 1950s. At that time a prominent conference president, Pastor Robert Greive, who had been president of the South Queensland Conference and at that time was president of the North New Zealand Conference, influenced a number of contemporaries of ours. Some of these were among the most outstanding students at Avondale College at the beginning of the 1950s. Together they left the Seventh-day Adventist Church, espousing many of the principles of Augustinian theology.

While it would be unfair to link Desmond Ford's defection entirely to these previous apostasies, nevertheless, one cannot doubt that they played an influential role. In the meantime, we cannot overlook the fact that some of the Augustinian heresies were being taught in our seminary, then located in Washington, D.C. For example, as early as 1947, at least one teacher has been reported as teaching the unfallen nature of Christ—a key issue in the *new theology*.[2]

By the 1950s, there was considerable anxiety concerning some of the teachers at the seminary. This was not because of the presentation of the concepts of the *new theology*, but rather because of their teaching of higher criticism. At this time, a number of these men were replaced by others who had been influenced by aspects of Augustinian theology. Because of their apparently deep Christ-centered approach and their apparent emphasis upon biblical theology, they were warmly welcomed as the answer to the dangerous errors taught by their predecessors. It took much time before the real nature of their theology was discovered. Error had been replaced by error.

It is significant to note that, at the end of the 1950s, Dr. Desmond Ford enrolled in the seminary, located then in Washington, D.C., and completed his master's degree there before proceeding to his doctorate at Michigan State University. Dr. Ford returned to Australia at the beginning of the 1960s, to head the Theology Department at Avondale College. This was the time when the impact of Robert Brinsmead was being sorely felt in Australia. Leadership was doing everything it could to counter his rapidly growing influence amongst conservative Adventists. They soon found in Desmond Ford a charismatic individual to counter Brinsmead's theology. Indeed, at that time, Brinsmead was true to basic, sound Adventist doctrine in almost all his views. However, as the sixties progressed, his increasing emphasis upon the Augustinian concept of original sin and the blotting out of unconscious sin at the sealing made him most vulnerable to

Evangelical Protestant theology. This accounted for his drastic change of direction in the early 1970s.

It is doubtful whether Dr. Ford relished his role as the defender of the church against Brinsmead, as both had been at Avondale College together and were on friendly terms. Because of Dr. Ford's defense of the church, few concerned themselves about the insidious theology he, himself, was preaching publicly. Nor did they detect the dangerous teachings he was presenting to his students at Avondale College.

However, by 1965, an alarming situation occurred, in which five interns from Avondale College attending the Victorian Conference camp meeting rose up against the presentation of the sanctuary message. Those presentations were given by one of the most outstanding and successful evangelists in the history of the church in Australia and New Zealand, Pastor George Burnside. Alarmed, Pastor Burnside, together with the conference president, Pastor Leo Rose, and the Trans-Commonwealth (now Trans-Australian) Union president, Pastor John Keith, reported their concerns to the division. At this time, neither leadership in the division nor in the college was prepared to see any problems in the theology of Dr. Ford, whom these interns had identified as the source of their opposition to the sanctuary message. Undoubtedly, Dr. Ford's key role in defending the church against Robert Brinsmead's views encouraged the church leadership in Australasia to ignore his aberrant views.

When Robert Brinsmead came under the direct influence of the Evangelical movement at the beginning of the 1970s, his theology, more and more, took on the garb of Evangelical teachings. Indeed, while there may have been some minor variations, his theological bases were then very close to those of Dr. Ford's.

It is our viewpoint that one of the great influences upon Dr. Ford was not simply the seminary, but the fact that he was an avid reader of the sermons of notable Scottish preachers. Very frequently he used these as the basis of his own sermonizing. Authored by members of the Church of Scotland, these sermons bore witness to Augustinian theology which is imbedded in Calvinistic teachings. Unquestionably, these Augustinian concepts were incorporated into the teachings of Dr. Ford.

In the early 1970s, Dr. Ford traveled to Manchester University, England, and there studied under F. F. Bruce, a renowned professor, and also a member, of the Plymouth Brethren faith. (The Plymouth Brethren Church was founded by John Darby in the 19th century. It was deeply rooted in Augustinian theology and the Jesuit futuristic interpretation of prophecy.)

For a period of sixteen years, Dr. Ford shaped the theology of the ministry of the Australasian Division (now the South Pacific Division). Only a handful of his theology students were able to discern the errors in his teaching. His charismatic personality, his brilliant oratory, his photographic memory were such that it was difficult for students not to be swept headlong into his theological concepts. Problems proliferated. Soon Dr. Ford's preaching, and later that of his students, influenced those teaching in the academies and colleges of the South Pacific Division. The children were taught the new views in their schools, and the church members were hearing them presented weekly in their pulpits. At the same time, Bible study was declining, and large numbers became lambs to the slaughter before the plausible presentation of these false shepherds.

But we must hasten to add that the *new theology* has not been confined to a particular continent. Indeed, the influence of Conradi over all of Europe has been so pervasive that probably not one European nation has not been infected by this deviation from the Seventh-day Adventist faith. In Africa and in Asia alike, because of the teachings of some American, Australian, and European missionaries and nationals who have studied in certain Western Seventh-day Adventist colleges, there is now an alarming spread of the *new theology* to these regions. While not as strongly seen in Latin America, it has still found its way into these areas. Rapidly it is enmeshing large numbers of Seventh-day Adventist members. In saying this, we want to pay tribute to the faithful teachers in our schools and colleges who have fought, and continue to fight, valiantly against the inroads of the *new theology* in God's church.

The *new theology* is a worldwide problem. It has been used by Satan in an endeavor to derail God's remnant church. We have confidence in the testimony of Ellen White that he will not succeed, but a huge number of God's people will sadly be lost as a result of the acceptance of this unscriptural theology.

Endnotes

[1]For a fascinating detailing of the history of the new theology in the Seventh-day Adventist Church, read *Adventism Challenged*, vols. 1 and 2, from Hartland Publications, by the same authors.

[2] See chapter 5.

This page intentionally left blank

3

Dealing with the New Theology

There is no question that the furor caused by the *new theology* caused tremendous alarm among leadership in the church. It was of such a magnitude in Australia that a number of conferences were held, both in Australia and in the United States, to seek a solution.[1] Eventually it was decided that the best interests of Australia would be served by transferring Dr. Desmond Ford, the leading proponent of the *new theology*, from Australia to the United States.

In 1977 Dr. Ford took up a post in the Religion Department of Pacific Union College, California. This move was not made without considerable warning from a number who knew Dr. Ford well. Both of us were among those who offered warnings. As early as October 1975, Colin warned the president of Pacific Union College that Dr. Ford could split the campus. Colin also warned one of the vice presidents of the General Conference who assured him that the problem was a simple one. He saw Ford as a big fish in a little pool in Australia. He believed that, when he would come to the United States, he would match minds with the outstanding scholars we have in the seminary and colleges. He would then become a little fish in a big pool. Colin's response did prove accurate.

"He will become a big fish in a big pool. There is no Seventh-day Adventist theological mind in America that can match his mind." It is unlikely that the vice president really believed what Colin said. But subsequent events confirmed the forecast. Russell provided similar warnings to visiting General Conference personnel in Australia. Many leaders did not recognize that the *new theology* was already widespread in the United States, though its true nature was not understood. It simply came to the surface under the mesmeric presentations of Dr. Ford. In many of our colleges, theologians, trained in the universities of apostate Christianity, were already teaching these errors as if they were God's truth. Thousands of our young people were beguiled.

We have lost hundreds of ministers, denominational workers, and thousands of church members due to the *new theology*. Perhaps an even greater concern is the fact that much higher numbers who live by the *new theology* are remaining in the church. Many have placed themselves in a position where it will be very difficult for them to accept the simple proclamation of the gospel presented in the Word of God and entrusted to the Seventh-day Adventist Church.

The whole issue was exacerbated by the Glacier View meetings in 1980. There Dr. Ford was given the opportunity to make a defense of his positions of prophetic interpretation in the presence of over a hundred church administrators and scholars. This followed the uncharacteristically frank declaration before a meeting of the Adventist Forum at Angwin, in which Dr. Ford denied ever believing the sanctuary message as presented by the Seventh-day Adventist Church. Literally hundreds of thousands of dollars were spent on this meeting; and, yet sadly, at Glacier View, the issue addressed, that of prophetic interpretation, represented only a small segment of the problem. The issues of the gospel, righteousness by faith, salvation, the nature of man, the human nature of Christ, the nature of sin, and other keys to Ford's aberrant views on prophetic interpretation were not directly addressed.

Indeed, it was commonly concluded by many that, though Dr. Ford deviated on the issue of prophetic interpretation, he had placed beautiful theological insights before our people on the issues of salvation, the gospel, and righteousness by faith. Nothing could have been further from the truth. Dr. Ford's entire theology was riddled with Augustinian error. It is impossible to hold truth on the doctrine of righteousness by faith while denying the sanctuary message.

When it was decided to remove Dr. Ford from denominational employment, the situation was exacerbated by public pronouncements, both in word and in writing, on both sides of the Pacific Ocean. These included material written in the prestigious *Ministry* magazine. In this magazine it was emphasized that the Glacier View meeting, while taking a firm stand against the prophetic interpretations of Dr. Ford, did not address the issue of righteousness by faith. Yet Dr. Ford's errant views of righteousness by faith underpinned this prophetic deviation. To fail to appreciate this fact was a most serious failure. But the magazine caused further damage by declaring that Dr. Ford had made wonderful contributions to the church on the doctrine of righteousness by faith. This showed a naive approach to theological consistency. It indicated that some of our leaders had little concept of the organization of the *new theology* and every theological issue it espoused. It also indicated that, no doubt unwittingly, some leaders were prepared to accept an admixture of truth and error. Again it needs to be emphasized that it is quite impossible to hold error on the sanctuary and yet be consistent with Scripture on righteousness by faith, for both are inextricably united. Though some leaders saw the issue clearly, it was a matter of deep concern that some did not perceive this fact.

Dr. Ford, in personal conversation, wholeheartedly agreed that, if he was incorrect in his prophetic interpretation, he was also wrong on his principles of salvation. He at least was not blind to this crucial relationship. Since Glacier View, little has been done to redress this dichotomy. As a result, it is highly probable that aspects of the *new theology* have permeated the thinking and the belief systems of the majority of the church pastors and church members. The tragedy is that most do not recognize this perilous situation and would strongly deny that they believe the *new theology*. This is not to say that these confused ones believe every aspect of Augustinian theology. Indeed, virtually none has actually accepted every aspect of it. For example, they have not accepted infant baptism or the issue of eternal burning hell. However, in the areas of predestination, once-saved-always-saved, the unfallen nature of Christ, original sin, and eternal security there are telltale signs of the *new theology* within the thinking and preaching of many within the Seventh-day Adventist Church. These views greatly distort truth and provide the foundation for the present impotence of the church in Western nations.

At the same time church leaders were dealing with the Ford issue they were vigorously opposing the teachings of Robert Brinsmead, another Australian who had been separated from the Seventh-day Adventist Church. He was teaching in the late 1950s and 1960s what he called the Awakening Message. This message focused upon the heavenly sanctuary work and the sealing ministry of Christ.

Early in the 1970s Brinsmead dramatically altered the thrust of his message. Accepting many teachings from Evangelical Protestantism, he found himself increasingly in harmony with the Augustinian positions that Ford espoused. It became quite obvious that it was difficult for leaders to entirely reject the theology of Dr. Ford because it had been used for more than a decade to oppose the teaching of Brinsmead in the late 1950s and 1960s. Yet it was clear that Brinsmead was *persona non grata;* and, therefore, he was much more readily opposed.

Of course, later in the 1970s, Brinsmead seemed intent upon putting distance between his positions and those of Ford's, and, therefore, became more outspoken in denouncing cardinal Seventh-day Adventist beliefs, such as obedience to God's law and Sabbath observance. Brinsmead's logical mind took him beyond Ford's stance.

Almost a decade after Glacier View, the church has failed to adequately address the issue of righteousness by faith. Both publications and presentations upon the 1888 message of righteousness by faith have frequently shown an alarming lack of true understanding of this message. Some authors have also set forth a dangerous revision of history, in an attempt to align the 1888 message with the *new theology* concepts of the unfallen nature of Christ and victoriousless living. Such efforts are plainly intellectual dishonesty of the worst sort. No trace of the *new theology* views is to be found in the 1888 message.

Many are not sure which Christ they serve. They are uncertain whether God has power to give them victory over sin or whether He does not. Further, they are not sure what sin is. They are vague on the significance of the sanctuary message and the investigative judgment. Sabbathkeeping has lost much of its purpose; and a general vagueness has settled over many in the church, which blurs the distinctiveness and the uniqueness of the final message for the world.

We must acknowledge, however, some of the monumental efforts in the early to middle 1970s to provide a strong scriptural basis for revival and reformation. Led by General Conference president, Elder Robert Pierson, the 1973 and 1974 annual councils focused upon the beautiful principles of righteousness by faith. These stirring messages were supported by strong appeals from *Review and Herald* editor, Elder Kenneth Wood, and a special righteousness by faith issue of the magazine was produced. Alarmingly, many rose up against these timely, Christ-centered appeals.

Until we honestly and faithfully address these issues, church members will continue to be confused and God's people cannot be united in truth and sanctification. Truth, Bible supported, must and will be re-established in the Seventh-day Adventist Church.

Endnote

[1] See *Adventism Challenged*, vol. 1, Hartland Publications for details of these conferences.

4

Legalism, the Scourge of Adventism

In spite of the clear Catholic roots of the *new theology*, it was common in the 1970s to refer to the Seventh-day Adventist message as Romanish and papal. It was confidently claimed that to link justification and sanctification together in the gospel was to deny the Protestant Reformation and to establish Catholic principles within the Seventh-day Adventist Church.

It is true that the Catholic Church taught that the gospel centered upon both justification and sanctification, whereas Reformational Protestantism was built primarily upon a gospel of justification alone. The accusations leveled against the Seventh-day Adventist message were based upon the deliberations at the Council of Trent. The Council of Trent, held 1545–1563, was convened in a desperate effort to counter the Protestant Reformation. Over the 18-year period of the council, the bishops discussed many issues, but few more vigorously than the issue of whether the gospel consisted of justification alone. Eventually, by a majority vote, the bishops voted to uphold the view that the gospel consisted of both justification *and* sanctification.

Many articulate supporters of the *new theology* presented this evidence as positive proof that those who hold to Fundamental Seventh-day Adventist concepts placed themselves in the Catholic tradition rather than the Protestant tradition. To many uninformed hearers, this proved to be convincing evidence in support of the *new theology*. What was never revealed was the bottom line of the findings of the bishops at the Council of Trent. Their concept of sanctification was altogether different from the concept of biblical sanctification. It was a totally works-oriented concept. To the Roman Catholic bishops, the issue of sanctification was the issue of the seven "sacred" sacraments—Mass, Holy Orders, Marriage, Baptism, Penance, Confirmation, and Final Unction. The decision of the bishops was the ultimate statement of a works gospel; a sanctification built upon sacramentalism.

This was exactly the legalism of the Jews condemned by Christ. It is the belief that works can merit salvation. Commenting on this, Ellen White said,

> Priests and rulers became fixed in a rut of ceremonialism. They were satisfied with a legal religion, and it was impossible for them to give to others the living truths of heaven (*Acts of the Apostles,* p. 15).

> A legal religion has been thought quite the correct religion for this time. But it is a mistake. . . . A cold, legal religion can never lead souls to Christ; for it is a loveless, Christless religion. . . . The solemn assembly for worship, the round of religious ceremonies, the external humiliation, the imposed sacrifice—all proclaim to the world a testimony that the doer of these things

can make himself righteous (*Selected Messages*, vol. 1, p. 388).

The Seventh-day Adventist Church has strongly disavowed this legalistic concept of salvation!

> It is impossible for us, of ourselves, to escape from the pit of sin in which we are sunken. Our hearts are evil, and we cannot change them. . . . Education, culture, the exercise of the will, human effort, all have their proper sphere, but here they are powerless. They may produce an outward correctness or behavior, but they cannot change the heart; they cannot purify the springs of life. There must be a power working from within, a new life from above, before men can be changed from sin to holiness. That power is Christ. His grace alone can quicken the lifeless faculties of the soul, and attract it to God and holiness (*Steps to Christ*, p. 18).

In the light of these and many other statements, it is plain that the Seventh-day Adventist Church has an entirely different concept of sanctification. The sanctification understood by faithful Seventh-day Adventists contains not one wit of legalism or merit of human worth. It is built upon a sanctification that is a gift from God through the sacrifice of Jesus Christ. Seventh-day Adventists constantly support the clearest testimony of Scripture that links justification and sanctification indivisibly together in the gospel. In so doing, they deny the ceremonialism and the sacramentalism of the Jews and the Catholic Church. True sanctification is by faith just as surely as justification is by faith.

> To open their eyes, and to turn them from darkness to light, and from the power of Satan unto God, that they may receive forgiveness of sins, and inheritance

> among them which are *sanctified by faith* that is in me (Acts 26:18, emphasis added).

Not only are both justification and sanctification by faith, but they are both merited through the sacrifice of Jesus.

> Husbands, love your wives, even as Christ also loved the church, and gave himself for it; That he might *sanctify* and cleanse it with the washing of water by the word, That he might present it to himself a glorious church, not having spot, or wrinkle, or any such thing; but that it should be holy and without blemish (Ephesians 5:25–27, emphasis added).

> Wherefore Jesus also, that he might *sanctify* the people with his own blood, suffered without the gate (Hebrews 13:12, emphasis added).

> By the which will we are *sanctified* through the offering of the body of Jesus Christ once for all (Hebrews 10:10, emphasis added).

Perceptive investigation of the *new theology* demonstrates that it has been established upon a legalistic concept of sanctification. Unlike the biblical concept which proclaims the fact that sanctification is by faith, the *new theology* has accepted a works-oriented definition of sanctification, built upon man's best efforts to respond to Christ's justifying grace. It is because of this that those who understand the power of the gospel to both justify and sanctify are misrepresented as believing that the gospel is faith plus works. Therefore faithful Seventh-day Adventists are erroneously referred to as legalists and perfectionists. Indeed, a clear understanding of the gospel shows that grace is provided for all by the salvation acts of Jesus.

In summary, it might be said that there are those who believe the gospel is justification by faith and sanctification by works. This belief was epidemic in Christ's day and later in the Roman Catholic Church. It has also been widespread amongst many Protestants, including Seventh-day Adventists. Such is Satan's counterfeit.

The *new theology* creates a second system of error by rejecting sanctification as part of the gospel. Because the holders of this view accept the Catholic view of sanctification as involving man's efforts, they feel correctly that this has no place in the gospel. But rather should these folk reject the unscriptural Catholic view of sanctification and espouse Christ's call to a holy life, which is entirely in His power and by His merits.

Finally there are those who believe the Bible testimony that the gospel is justification and sanctification by faith. This was the unwavering testimony of Ellen White throughout her ministry. This is the glorious gospel of the three angels' messages which God has asked us to proclaim to the world.

It is important to acknowledge that many Seventh-day Adventists have truly been imprisoned by legalism. The testimony of Sister White is specific in indicating that the unity of the law and the gospel had frequently not been preached. We had preached the law so strongly that we had well-nigh lost sight of Jesus, the One who alone provides the power for victorious living (*Testimonies to Ministers,* p. 94; *Selected Messages,* vol. 3, p. 172). Sister White also concluded that we had not preached the commandments of God and the faith of Jesus with equal force (*Selected Messages,* vol. 3, p. 184). It was as if we had proclaimed the law of God with a loud voice but the faith of Jesus in a whisper.

It was understandable that these earnest preachers of the early Seventh-day Adventist Church had expended much effort proclaiming the binding nature of the law because it had been neglected by mainstream Protestants. But it was tragic that the faith of Jesus had not been given equal emphasis. We cannot keep the law of God except we have the faith of Jesus.

Certainly legalism has not been confined to the pre-1888 era. It has been, and will continue to be, a constant threat to the remnant church. Only a focusing upon Jesus Christ and a full surrender to Him can avoid this fatal error. The problem of the legalist is that he can never keep the law, for he has not appropriated the only power by which he can keep the law. Thus the legalist is of all men most miserable. Daily he faces the desire and acknowledgement that *he must keep the law to be saved.* Yet his honest evaluation leads him to realize his constant failures. This is the ground of frustration, neuroticism, helplessness, and hopelessness. Thus, constantly, we must uphold the matchless love and power of Christ before our people.

It is evident that the *new theology* attempted to redress the spiritual cancer of legalism. But its solution was as eternally destructive as was legalism itself. There was one difference, however. Those who saw the *new theology* emphasis upon relational Christianity (i.e., it's not my performance that counts but it is my relationship to Jesus Christ) emphasized the love but said little about the power. Focusing upon a "justification alone" gospel, they accepted a deadly concept that God's people will continue to sin until Jesus returns. The adherents of the *new theology*, however, do not share the helpless frustration of the legalist and, indeed, live in a euphoria of salvation when, indeed, they are destruction bound. Because of this delusion, they may be in an even more perilous state then the legalist, who in honesty must acknowledge his failure to be ready to meet Jesus.

The gospel of Christ allows neither the barrenness of legalism nor the powerlessness of the *new theology*. It encompasses both the forgiveness and the spiritual restoration of man into the image of his Creator. Like inseparable Siamese twins, it binds together the law and the gospel; the commandments of God and the faith of Jesus; truth and love; justification and sanctification. This was the message of 1888 that would have led to the outpouring of the latter rain, the giving of the loud cry, and the return of Jesus to take His faithful children home. It is the message that will bring in everlasting righteousness in our lifetime, if we accept it.

This page was intentionally left blank.

5

The Human Nature of Christ and the New Theology

With his academic dean, Dr. Jack Blanco, Colin had been talking with Elder Kenneth Wood and Dr. Herbert Douglass, editor and associate editor, respectively, of the *Review and Herald* (now known as the *Adventist Review*). Both were emphatic. They believed that the human nature of Christ was the real key to the theological controversy in the Seventh-day Adventist Church. The year was 1974. They had been talking about the worrisome theological schisms in Australia.

We had been brought up in Australia. We learned both in home and school that Christ had the nature of fallen man, but it didn't seem a significant issue, and we had not studied it carefully.

Well, we remember the first time that we questioned the nature of Christ. We were about 8 years old. As was common, we were in serious trouble with our mother; and she had asked why it was that we could not be like Jesus when He was a boy? Colin retorted, "How was it that Jesus did not sin?" To the best of our recollection, our mother replied, "The Holy Spirit overshadowed Him." We remember thinking, I wish the Holy Spirit would overshadow us. Of course, we had no idea that we were asking a deep theological question that was to engross the attention and the polemics of the Seventh-day Adventist Church later in our lifetime.

In 1966, while traveling with a fellow colleague from Avondale College, the colleague insisted that Christ had an unfallen nature. While Colin could not agree with him, on the other hand, he did not see it as a major issue. After all, the only important issue, he thought, was that Christ's sacrifice was effective for him; and, surely, that was all that needed to be addressed.

Little did Colin perceive the depth of the issues at stake. It was because of the statements of Elder Wood and Dr. Douglass, eight years later, that he decided he must study the issue. His dean indicated that he, too, had not deeply studied the issue, and he would study. After five weeks of intense study, Colin came to the conviction that, indeed, Elder Wood and Dr. Douglass were correct.

One Friday, at lunch time, Colin explained his newfound convictions to his dean. He was thrilled to discover that Dr. Blanco also had been studying the subject of the human nature of Christ, and had come to similar convictions. Then and there they knelt down to thank God for leading them together to truth. Since then, deeper and fuller insights into the beautiful truth of the incarnation of our Lord have come to us, and we are convinced that throughout eternity this will be one of the most fruitful studies in which God's people will be engaged.

The issue of the human view of Jesus Christ has heightened as we have reached the centennial of the 1888 Minneapolis General Conference. Because there are no official transcripts of the messages of Dr. Ellet Waggoner and Elder Alonzo Jones, we cannot be sure of the exact content of the messages that they preached at the conference. However, we can be sure that very shortly afterwards the messages of both, and especially Jones, were centered upon the fallen human nature of Jesus Christ. In Jones' book, *The Consecrated Way to Christian Perfection,* he devotes 11 of the 17 chapters to the subject of Christ as our heavenly High Priest, exploring the scriptural evidence for the fallen human nature of Jesus. Though published in 1905, it varied little from Jones' discourses in the early 1890s.

There has been a-none-too-subtle attempt to undermine the Bible truth on the human nature of Christ by indicating that this emphasis of Jones and Waggoner was a result of progressive apostasy in what they believed. That this is not true is evidenced by the fact that there is no extant letter from the servant of the Lord rebuking them or counseling them in respect of this teaching. On the other hand, we have letter after letter that was written by Sister White, in an attempt to help them in other areas of their presentations when Sister White recognized that they were losing the beauty of the message that they had presented.

More importantly, the writings of Sister White, herself, are full of unequivocal statements supporting the central truth of the fallen human nature of Jesus Christ. Those who believe in the unfallen (prelapsarian) view of the nature of Christ frequently resort to statements such as, "The church has not taken a stand on the nature of Christ." Based upon this dubious statement, they draw one of two conclusions: 1. The human nature of Christ should never be explored in preaching because there is no official pronouncement by the church. 2. We can preach and teach either way without violating the principles of church authority.

Both viewpoints can be dangerous.

The first view is dangerous because the Seventh-day Adventist Church was not predicated upon the primacy of the church, but of the Word. As growing lads, we remember frequently hearing such statements as "The Bible and the Bible only is our rule of faith and practice." "We have no creed but the Bible." "The Bible is the only arbiter of truth." The concept that the church possessed final authority on the issue of doctrine was always considered to be a deadly papal error. Furthermore, Inspiration emphasizes how central the study of Christ's humanity should be to all of us.

> The humanity of the Son of God is everything to us. It is the golden chain that binds our souls to Christ, and through Christ to God. This is to be our study. . . . When we approach this subject, we would do well to heed the words spoken by Christ to Moses at the burning bush, "Put off thy shoes from off thy feet, for the place where on thou standeth is holy ground" (Exodus 3:5).

> We should come to this study with the humility of a learner, with a contrite heart. And the study of the incarnation of Christ is a fruitful field, which will repay the searcher who digs deep for hidden truth (*Selected Messages*, vol. 1, p. 244).

The second view, which asserts that we are free to preach and teach either view on the nature of Christ, assumes that we are free to accept pluralism. It opens the door to the belief that it is a matter of small concern whether we teach truth or error. This well serves Satan's purposes. God deals only with absolute truth.

Another claim of those propounding the *new theology* is to assert that Sister White supports both sides of the issue. To suggest this gives Sister White a "wax nose." But God never inspires His servants to present contradictory messages. Frequently men will misuse Sister White's statements in order to make it appear that she spoke on both sides of the question. This shameful distortion of truth is also applied by skeptics to certain biblical references. Only the biblically naive are influenced by such unholy techniques.

In his monumental work, *The Word Was Made Flesh,*[1] Dr. Ralph Larson investigated every written work published by the Seventh-day Adventist Church in the United States, Great Britain, South Africa, and Australia, from the year 1852 when the first published reference to the nature of Christ appeared. Elder Larson discovered that, from 1852 to 1952, approximately 1,200 statements appeared in our publications, dealing with the subject of the human nature of Christ. Of these, there were approximately four hundred written by Sister White and eight hundred authored by other writers. Without fail, when reference was made to the humanity of Jesus, the authors upheld the doctrine of His fallen nature.

After 1952, in what Dr. Larson calls the "Epoch of Confusion," insidious new elements have caused confusion and dissension in the Seventh-day Adventist Church. In our own investigation, we have discovered that, as early as 1947, the Adventist Theological Seminary, which was then located in

Washington, D.C., had at least one teacher on its faculty who was teaching the error of the unfallen nature of Christ. When, in the middle of the 1950s, the book, *Questions on Doctrine*, was published, in one full sweep, the authors sought to present, as orthodox within the Seventh-day Adventist Church, this aberrant view that finds its origin in Augustinian Catholicism. Probably no book has caused more anguish to the Seventh-day Adventist Church than this book.

For the last four decades, the prevailing teaching in our colleges and seminaries (with a few notable exceptions) has led in this direction. Therefore, a whole generation of ministers, through no fault of their own, have been led away from the beautiful truths of the humanity of Jesus Christ. Yet, today, there are many ministers who have recognized the error of this doctrine and have joined the ranks of those who are again preaching the biblical message of the fallen nature of our Lord and Saviour. Through this beautiful truth, Jesus shines forth with new luster to the minds of men and women.

Some of the reasons we understand that Christ took man's fallen nature are as follows:

1. The least important is the fact that historically the Seventh-day Adventist Church has preached the fallen nature.

2. We have to accept the fallen nature because the Bible supports it.

> For we have not an high priest which cannot be touched with the feeling of our infirmities; but *was in all points tempted like as we are*, yet without sin (Hebrews 4:15, emphasis added).

Forasmuch then as the children are partakers of flesh and blood, he also himself likewise took part of the same; that through death he might destroy him that had the power of death, that is the devil; and deliver them who through fear of death were all their lifetime subject to bondage. For verily he took not on him the nature of angels; but *he took on him the seed of Abraham*. Wherefore *in all things it behoved him to be made like unto his brethren*, that he might be a merciful and faithful high priest in things pertaining to God, to make reconciliation for the sins of the people. For in that he himself hath suffered being tempted, he is able to succor them that are tempted (Hebrews 2:14–18, emphasis added).

Concerning his Son Jesus Christ our Lord, which was *made of the seed of David* according to the flesh (Romans 1:3, emphasis added).

For what the law could not do, in that it was weak through the flesh, *God sending his own Son in the likeness of sinful flesh*, and for sin, condemned sin in the flesh: That the righteousness of the law might be fulfilled in us, who walk not after the flesh, but after the Spirit (Romans 8:3, 4, emphasis added).

But when the fulness of the time was come, God sent forth his Son, *made of a woman, made under the law*, To redeem them that were under the law, that we might receive the adoption of sons (Galatians 4:4, 5).

3. There are over 40 statements in which the issue of the human nature of Christ is specifically addressed by Sister White. Always she refers to the human nature of Christ as "fallen" or "sinful," thus confirming the words of Scripture. Never once does she use the term "unfallen" or "sinless" in relation to Christ's human nature. These statements include:

Letters have been coming into me, affirming that Christ could not have had the same nature as man, for if He had, He would have fallen under similar temptations. If He did not have man's nature, He could not be our example. If He was not a partaker of our nature, He could not have been tempted as man has been (*Selected Messages*, vol. 1, p. 408).

The great work of redemption could be carried out only by the Redeemer taking the place of *fallen* Adam (*Review and Herald*, February 24, 1874, emphasis added).

Not withstanding that the sins of a guilty world were laid upon Christ, not withstanding the humiliation of taking upon Himself our *fallen* nature, the voice from heaven declared Him to be the Son of the Eternal (*Desire of Ages*, p. 112, emphasis added).

He would take man's *fallen* nature (*Early Writings*, p. 150, emphasis added).

It was in the order of God that Christ should take upon Himself the form and *nature of fallen man* (*Spiritual Gifts*, vol. 4, p. 115, emphasis added).

When Adam was assailed by the tempter, none of the effects of sin were upon him. He stood in the strength of perfect manhood, possessing the full vigor of mind and body. He was surrounded with the glories of Eden, and was in daily communion with heavenly beings. *It was not thus with Jesus* when He entered the wilderness to cope with Satan. For four thousand years the race had been decreasing in *physical strength*, in *mental power*, and in *moral worth*; and *Christ took upon Him the affirmities of degenerate humanity*. Only thus could He rescue man from the lowest depths of degradation (*Desire of Ages*, p. 117, emphasis added).

Perhaps the most poignant expression of Sister White upon this matter states that Christ *took* our sinful nature.

> He took upon His sinless nature our sinful nature, that He might know how to succorr those that are tempted (*Medical Ministry*, p. 181).

Some have attempted to support the view that Jesus simply took the physical form alone, but that cannot be sustained by the evidence in Sister White's writings (reread *Spiritual Gifts*, vol. 4, p. 115).

To separate Christ's physical nature from His mental and moral nature would take us both to the Greek pagan concept of the distinction between an evil body and a good soul. No right thinking Seventh-day Adventist dare accept that dualistic view of man. It is a satanic deception. If Christ had a fallen physical nature, and He did, then His entire nature was fallen.

Some have emphasized the fact that Romans 8:3 uses the term,"*likeness* of sinful flesh." When we realize that the word here, translated "likeness," is the same Greek word, *homoiomo*, from which we derive the word, *homogeneity* (of the same order), we do not need to stumble over this. Paul's use of this Greek word is illustrated below.

> But made himself of no reputation, and took upon him the form of a servant, and was made in the *likeness* of men (Philippians 2:7, emphasis added).

No one would use this text to prove that Christ was *unlike* men. Yet such poor logic is frequently applied to Romans 8:3. Consistency and good logic would preclude "likeness" there being interpretated "unlikeness."

Where some of us have made mistakes in the past is that we have not addressed the genuine concerns of those who honestly hold to the pre-Fall view of Christ's nature. Such are also addressing passages of the Bible and the Spirit of Prophecy. The two most common texts that are used in support of this error are Luke 1:35 and Hebrews 7:26.

> And the angel answered and said unto her, the Holy Ghost shall come upon thee, and the power of the Highest shall overshadow thee: therefore also that *holy thing* which shall be born of thee shall be called the Son of God (Luke 1:35, emphasis added).

> For such an high priest became us, who is *holy, harmless, undefiled, separate from sinners*, and made higher than the heavens (Hebrews 7:26, emphasis added).

It is important here to realize that these scriptures are not talking about *nature*, that which we inherited, but *character*. A clear distinction between nature and character avoids the anomalous view of some, suggesting that Christ had both the pre-Fall and post-Fall natures. It may be significant that every Jewish eldest male child was called "holy unto the Lord."

> As it is written in the law of the Lord, Every male that openeth the womb shall be called holy to the Lord (Luke 2:23).

Some have been concerned that those who believe in the post-Fall nature of Christ (postlapsarian) are making Christ a sinner. This has been exacerbated by the fact that so many of those who espouse these concerns believe in a modified form of Augustinian original sin. Their argument states that if Christ was born with a sinful nature, He was automatically a sinner. This is an argument that S. N. Haskell had to meet back at the turn of the century when he had been detailed to help those who were affected by the holy flesh movement in Indiana. In writing to Sister White on the topic, he said,

> When we stated that we believe that Christ was born in fallen humanity, they [the holy flesh people] would represent us as believing that Christ sinned, notwithstanding the fact that we would state our position so clearly that it would seem as if no one could misunderstand us. Their point of theology in this particular respect seemed to be this: They believe that Christ took Adam's nature before he fell (S. N. Haskell, letter to Ellen White, Sept. 25, 1900).

A number of statements made by Sister White, taken almost exclusively from a letter she wrote to Pastor W.L.H. Baker in 1895, have been used to support the pre-Fall view of the nature of Christ. This letter is set out in some detail in the fifth volume of the *Bible Commentary* and in full in Dr. Ralph Larson's book. The concepts expressed there that have been misunderstood include:

> Do not set Him [Christ] before the people as a man with the propensities of sin (*Bible Commentary*, vol. 5, p. 1128).

In this message, we are warned against asserting that Christ had *propensities of sin.* At the same time, Sister White expresses the fact that we are born with inherent propensities of disobedience. Also, she warns against making Christ exactly like us. However, here she is talking again about His character, not His nature.

Perhaps the most explicit expression of this fact is as follows:

> Jesus Christ is our example in all things. He began life, passed through its experiences, and ended its record, with a sanctified human will. He was tempted in all points like as we are, and yet because He kept His will surrendered and sanctified, He never bent in the slightest degree towards the doing of evil, or towards manifesting rebellion against God (Special Testimonies, Oct. 29, 1894).

Here surely is the key. The whole difference between Christ and man was not nature but character. That one understanding of the human nature of Christ enhances our understanding of the gift of Heaven. It helps us to understand what it really meant for God to give His only begotten Son that whosoever believeth in Him should not perish, but have everlasting life (John 3:16). It helps us to understand how Jesus is able to succor them that are tempted (Hebrews 2:17) and why He is not willing that any should perish, but that all should come to repentance (2 Peter 3:9). We begin to understand how He is able to save to the uttermost all that come unto God by Him (Hebrews 7:25).

In using the Baker letter in defense of the error that Jesus took an unfallen human nature, men are simply wresting Inspiration. It will be noted that the quoted passage does not plainly state that Jesus possessed an unfallen human nature. It rather addresses the fact that He possessed no propensities of sin. This is a markedly difficult matter. Yet proponents of the *new theology* would have us equate the absence of propensities of sin with the possession of a unfallen nature. It is no such thing. That this is so is proven by the fact that:

> We need not retain one sinful propensity (*Bible Commentary*, vol. 7, p. 943).

Since we manifestly do possess fallen natures, it is undeniable that the absence of sinful propensities may be a characteristic of individuals possessing such a nature. Thus to use the Baker letter as proof that Christ possessed an unfallen nature demonstrates a failure to fully investigate the matter.

Many equate sinful propensities with the temptations they experience. Yet Jesus was tempted in all points like as we are. Thus this is a false conclusion. Sister White cites examples of sinful propensities. These prove to be evil attributes of character; thus verifying that the statement in the Baker letter testifies to the fact that Christ possessed a sinless character, despite possessing the disadvantage of our fallen natures. Only thus could He truly be our Example. The relevant passage states:

> Self-indulgence, self-pleasing, pride, and extravagance must be renounced. We cannot be Christians and gratify these propensities (*Review and Herald*, May 16, 1893).

No one addresses the humanity of Christ more fully than does the apostle John. No doubt, because he was exposing the gnostic errors of his day, he both affirmed the divinity and the humanity of Jesus Christ.

> In the beginning was the Word, and the Word was with God, and the Word was God. The same was in the beginning with God (John 1:1, 2).

> And the Word was made flesh, and dwelt among us, (and we beheld his glory, the glory as of the only begotten of the Father,) full of grace and truth (John 1:14).

> That which was from the beginning, which we have heard, which we have seen with our eyes, which we

have looked upon, and our hands have handled, of
the Word of life; (For the life was manifested, and we
have seen it, and bear witness, and shew unto you
that eternal life, which was with the Father, and was
manifested unto us) (1 John 1:1, 2).

This is the same John who offers the most pointed evidence
of the importance of the issue of the nature of Christ:

Hereby know ye the Spirit of God: Every spirit that
confesseth that Jesus Christ is come in the flesh is of
God: and every spirit that confesseth not that Jesus
Christ is come in the flesh is not of God: and this is
that spirit of antichrist, whereof ye have heard that it
should come; and even now already is it in the world
(1 John 4:2, 3).

It is thus evident that the human nature of Christ is central
to the identification of the antichrist. As Seventh-day Adventists, in line with Wycliffe, Luther, and the other Reformers,
we have no question of the modern-day application of the
antichrist to the papacy. The Catholic Church upholds the
doctrine that Christ had an unfallen nature, denying that
Christ came to earth with the nature of sinful flesh. This
insight of John soberly focuses the issue within the context
of the great controversy.

John further emphasized this matter:

For many deceivers are entered into the world, who
confess not that Jesus Christ is come in the flesh. This
is a deceiver and an antichrist (2 John 7).

The key doctrinal error of the papacy (antichrist) is here
cited to be the belief that Jesus did not come in the flesh. This
manifestly cannot refer to a belief that Jesus was not human,
for the papacy has never denied that fact. But, with its
doctrine of the Immaculate Conception, the papacy has

denied the truth that Jesus came with our fallen nature. Here is the core of the spirit of antichrist; and here, too, is the core of the *new theology*. They are dangerous bedfellows.

Paul gives strong support to this interpretation in his identification of the mystery of godliness (1 Timothy 3:16) and the mystery of iniquity (2 Thessalonians 2:7). An understanding of the mystery of godliness is essential to our understanding of the mystery of iniquity. Paul declares the human nature of Christ to be central to the mystery of godliness:

> And without controversy great is the mystery of godliness: *God was manifest in the flesh*, justified in the Spirit, seen of angels, preached unto the Gentiles, believed on in the world, received up into glory (1 Timothy 3:16, emphasis added).

If Christ's coming in fallen human flesh is the key to our understanding of the mystery of godliness; then, surely, the key to our understanding of the mystery of iniquity is the denial that Jesus came in the flesh. This is why John refers to this error, as the spirit of antichrist.

The insights of Paul upon the mystery of godliness and the mystery of iniquity unlock the central relationship of the human nature of Christ to character perfection. Those who believe Christ was manifest in the flesh in fallen human nature understand the godliness that Christ provides for all who in faith accept Him.

Peter so perceptively understood the relationship between the nature of Christ and the mystery of godliness:

> Forasmuch then as Christ hath suffered for us in the flesh, arm yourselves likewise with the same mind: for he that hath suffered in the flesh hath ceased from sin. That he no longer should live the rest of his time in

the flesh to the lusts of men, but to the will of God (1
Peter 4:1, 2).

Those who deny that Christ was manifest in the flesh run
the great risk that they will fall into iniquity. The very
thought that Christ is apart from us with an altogether different nature provides an excuse for their sin. How essential,
then, it is that we reverently study the humanity of Christ on
our knees, accepting the wondrous understanding that in
human weakness He appropriated the power of His Father
to turn back the temptations of Satan. The deeper we study
the humanity of Jesus, the more it will unlock, for our lives,
the mystery of godliness.

In conclusion, we would want to offer some solemn counsel. It is easy to understand the nature of Christ within the
polemics of strife and contention. It is easy to place it within
the realm of argumentative and debative theology. This is a
great message, critical to our understanding of the sanctuary
message, to our understanding of the great power of God to
give to all, who will surrender, victory over sin in the life,
and critical to our ability to preach Revelation 14:12 with
power and conviction.

We must see this message in the light of the total salvation
acts of God, through His Son, Jesus Christ. We must see all
this in the light of Calvary. It is not difficult to place labels on
those who have different concepts from our own. But we
have discovered in our dialogues with many ministers that,
as we have carefully explained the difference between nature
and character, there has frequently been a wonderful understanding that, while we are recognizing that Christ has the
same nature as ours, we are emphasising the truth that He

has an altogether different character. Yet the comforting news is that He wants to enshrine that character in your life and ours. Offered to us is the power of the One who alone walked this earth without blemish.

> Let this mind be in you which was also in Christ Jesus (Philippians 2:5).

> He is able "to present you faultless before the presence of His Father" (Jude 24).

> God . . . will not suffer you to be tempted above that ye are able; but will with the temptation also make a way to escape, . . . (1 Corinthians 10:13).

Through His promises we may "be partakers of the divine nature, having escaped the corruption that is in the world through lust" (2 Peter 1:4).

He is the one who teaches us that "denying ungodliness and worldly lusts, we should live soberly, righteously, and godly, *in this present world*" (Titus 2:12, emphasis added).

The truth of the incarnation of Jesus enriches our understanding of God's last message to the church of Laodicea. The promise to the overcomer rings with a new meaning.

> To him that overcometh will I grant to sit with me in my throne, *even as I also overcame,* and am set down with my Father in his throne (Revelation 3:21, emphasis added).

As we understand and respond to the fullness of the humiliation of our Lord in both clothing His divinity with our humanity and suffering the shame of the cross, our stony hearts are broken. When we fully understand this great truth and respond to the matchless love of God, our hearts are transformed as the things of this world grow strangely dim in the light of His glory and grace.

Endnote

[1]Dr. Ralph Larson, *The Word Made Flesh*, Cherrystone Press, 1986.

6

The Nature of Man and the New Theology

The *new theology* is predicated upon erroneous views on the nature of man. Indeed, this is one of the principal areas in which the *new theology* may be identified. Seven cardinal tenants will be examined in the light of God's Word.

1. *Man is not born with original sin.* The concept of original sin was firmly etched in the Augustinian concepts of Christianity. He brought this notion with him from paganism. This concept holds that man is born, and even conceived, guilty because of Adam's sin. There is nothing that man can do nor God does to rectify this situation. This false pretense leads many to believe that God alone arbitrarily preordains some to eternal salvation. Others, He determines, will suffer eternal punishment. Some Christians cite the prayer of repentance offered by David, as evidence for this view. Often modern translations are quoted. In many of these translations, there is a slanting of the translation to reflect the translator's bias towards original sin. In the King James Version, one such text reads as follows:

> Behold, I was shapen in iniquity; and in sin did my mother conceive me (Psalm 51:5).

However, in the interpretive translation of the New International Version, this same text is biased toward original sin.

> Surely I have been a sinner from birth, sinful from
> the time my mother conceived me (Psalm 51:5, NIV).

This text, in the Hebrew, says nothing about guilt or original sin. The subsequent verses set forth the truth that it was possible for David to be totally cleansed from the sin that he had committed with Bathsheba:

> Behold, thou desirest truth in the inward parts: and
> in the hidden part thou shalt make me to know wisdom. Purge me with hissop, and I shall be clean: wash
> me, and I shall be whiter than snow (Psalm 51:6, 7).

> Create in me a clean heart, O God; and renew a
> right spirit within me (Psalm 51:10).

These texts dispel any thought that David believed in original sin or its corollary that man cannot cease from sin. God's truth, however, indicates that man is born with evil tendencies, with natural inclinations to move in pathways that alienate from God. Unconverted man will naturally become a sinner and be separated from God.

The Bible emphasizes that a man is responsible for his own sin, not for the sin of someone else:

> And the Lord said unto Moses, Whosoever hath
> sinned against me, him will I blot out of my book (Exodus 32:33).

> The soul that sinneth, it shall die. The son shall not
> bear the iniquity of the father, neither shall the father
> bear the iniquity of the son: the righteousness of the
> righteous shall be upon him, and the wickedness of
> the wicked shall be upon him (Ezekiel 18:20).

These inspired texts emphatically deny the false doctrine of original sin. In no manner does God hold men guilty of the sin of their forefathers. If original sin were biblical, then God would not have declared concerning John the Baptist,

> For he shall be great in the sight of the Lord, and shall drink neither wine nor strong drink; and *he shall be filled with the Holy Ghost*, even from his mother's womb (Luke 1:15, emphasis added).

We are guilty because of our own sin:

> For all have sinned, and come short of the glory of God (Romans 3:23).

> Wherefore, as by one man sin entered into the world, and death by sin; and so death passed upon all men *for that all have sinned*: (Romans 5:12, emphasis added).

2. *Man's eternity is not predestined by God.* It is true that only a few Seventh-day Adventists would openly espouse the predestinarian doctrine. However, by implication, the acceptance of the concept of original sin logically predisposes one to this conclusion as it did Luther and Calvin. Yet the Scriptures emphatically declare that man chooses his own eternal destiny:

> And if it seem evil unto you to serve the Lord, choose you this day whom ye will serve; whether the gods which your fathers served that were on the other side of the of the flood, or the gods of the Amorites, in whose land ye dwell: but as for me and my house, we will serve the Lord (Joshua 24:15).

> O Jerusalem, Jerusalem, thou that killest the prophets, and stonest them which are sent unto thee, how often would I have gathered thy children

together, even as a hen gathereth her chickens under
her wings, and ye would not (Matthew 23:37)!

And the Spirit and the bride say, Come. And let
him that heareth say, Come. And let him that is athirst
come. And whosoever will, let him take the water of
life freely (Revelation 22:17).

Christ drew all men unto Himself by His death on Calvary (John 12:32), but man is free to accept or reject this
purchased salvation.

3. *Man's salvation is conditional.* Many Seventh-day Adventists are unaware that the evil doctrine of once-saved-
always-saved is associated with the *new theology*. This is
due to the fact that it is introduced in a more subtle form
than that presented by most Evangelical Protestants. Yet
those who believe that we will be saved irrespective of victory over sin are implicitly espousing the once-saved-always-saved doctrine. The tacit implication of such a view is
that salvation is not conditional upon obedience. Yet the
Bible repeatedly asserts this to be so.

Now the just shall live by faith: but if any man
draw back, my soul shall have no pleasure in him
(Hebrews 10:38).

But when the righteous turneth away from his
righteousness, and committeth iniquity, and doeth according to all the abominations that the wicked man
doeth, shall he live? All his righteousness that he hath
done shall not be mentioned: in his trespass that he
hath trespassed, and in his sin that he hath sinned, in
them shall he die (Ezekiel 18:24).

For God so loved the world, that he gave his only
begotten Son, that whosoever believeth in him should
not perish, but have everlasting life (John 3:16).

Blessed is the man that endureth temptation: for when he is tried, he shall receive the crown of life, which the Lord hath promised to them that love him (James 1:12).

Harken, my beloved brethren, Hath not God chosen the poor of this world rich in faith, and heirs of the kingdom which he hath promised to them that love him (James 2:5)?

But the mercy of the LORD is from everlasting to everlasting upon them that fear him, and his righteousness unto children's children; to such as keep his covenant, and to those that remember his commandments to do them (Psalm 103:17, 18).

But if we walk in the light, as he is in the light, we have fellowship one with another, and the blood of Jesus Christ his Son cleanseth us from all sin (1 John 1:7).

And, behold, one came and said unto him, Good Master, what good thing shall I do, that I may have eternal life? And he said unto him, Why callest thou me good? there is none good but one, that is, God: but if thou wilt enter into life, keep the commandments (Matthew 19:16, 17).

4. *Christian character perfection is a gift from Jesus.* The *new theology* denies Christian *perfection*. The Bible upholds the privilege of all Christians to develop perfect characters. The proponents of the *new theology* confuse perfection with *perfectionism*. This latter concept accepts the satanic error that man's good works possess merit. But the Word of God says,

For by grace are ye saved through faith; and that not of yourselves: it is the gift of God (Ephesians 2:8).

Therefore we conclude that a man is justified by faith without the deeds of the law (Romans 3:28).

Knowing that a man is not justified by the works of the law, but by the faith of Jesus Christ, even we have believed in Jesus Christ, that we might be justified by the faith of Christ, and not by the works of the law: for by the works of the law shall no flesh be justified (Galatians 2:16).

Further, implicit within the concept of perfectionism, is the assertion that a man may reach a state beyond which no further progress is possible, a state of so-called "absolute perfection." It is claimed that he cannot fall from this state. Such beliefs are alien to God's Word and, thus, must be rejected. However, the Bible is replete with evidence that, in the power of Jesus, God's saints will be perfect:

And the Lord said unto Satan, Hast thou considered my servant Job, that there is none like him in the earth, a perfect and an upright man, one that feareth God, and escheweth evil (Job 1:8)?

Whosoever believeth that Jesus is the Christ is born of God: and every one that loveth him that begat loveth him also that is begotten of him. By this we know that we love the children of God, when we love God, and keep his commandments. For this is the love of God, that we keep his commandments: and his commandments are not grievous. For whatsoever is born of God overcometh the world: and this is the victory that overcometh the world, even our faith. Who is he that overcometh the world, but he that believeth that Jesus is the Son of God (1 John 5:1-5)?

And hereby we do know that we know him, if we keep his commandments. He that saith, I know him, and keepeth not his commandments, is a liar, and the truth is not in him. But whoso keepeth his word, in him verily is the love of God perfected: hereby know we that we are in him. He that saith he abideth in him ought himself also so to walk, even as he walked (1 John 2:3-6).

Be ye therefore perfect, even as your Father which is in heaven is perfect (Matthew 5:48).

Blessed are they that keep his testimonies, and that seek him with the whole heart. They also do no iniquity: they walk in his ways (Psalm 119:2, 3).

The remnant of Israel shall not do iniquity, nor speak lies; neither shall a deceitful tongue be found in their mouth (Zephaniah 3:13).

Whosoever is born of God doth not commit sin; for his seed remaineth in him: and he cannot sin, because he is born of God (1 John 3:9).

And he gave some, apostles; and some, prophets; and some, evangelists; and some, pastors and teachers; for the perfecting of the saints, for the work of the ministry, for the edifying of the body of Christ: Till we all come in unity of the faith, and of the knowledge of the Son of God, unto a perfect man, unto the measure of the stature of the fulness of Christ (Ephesians 4:11-13).

FORASMUCH then as Christ hath suffered for us in the flesh, arm yourselves likewise with the same mind: for he that hath suffered in the flesh hath ceased from sin; that he no longer should live the rest of his time in the flesh to the lusts of men, but to the will of God (1 Peter 4:1, 2).

Perfection is not accomplished by man, even by his best efforts. There will always be a battle, a march, and a struggle. But the perfecting of the character is the work of Christ. It is He alone who removes all sin from our lives. Perfection, however, is not maturity. The converted man or woman ever grows in the maturity of God's progressive revelations.

5. *The saints are provided Christ's victorious power to overcome sin.* The biblical truth accepted by faithful Seventh-day Adventists is that the saints can and will have victory over sin now. The *new theology* teaches that the saints continue to sin until Jesus comes. Scripture has this to say:

> Now unto him that is able to keep you from falling, and to present you faultless before the presence of his glory with exceeding joy (Jude 24).

> There hath no temptation taken you but such as is common to man: but God is faithful, who will not suffer you to be tempted above that ye are able; but will with the temptation also make a way to escape, that ye may be able to bear it (1 Corinthians 10:13).

> I can do all things through Christ which strengtheneth me (Philippians 4:13).

> That he might present it to himself a glorious church, not having spot, or wrinkle, or any such thing; but that it should be holy and without blemish (Ephesians 5:27).

> But God, who is rich in mercy, for his great love wherewith he loved us, even when we were dead in sins, hath quickened us together with Christ, (by grace ye are saved;) and hath raised us up together, and made us sit together in heavenly places in Christ Jesus (Ephesians 2:4-6).

> Awake to righteousness, and sin not; for some have not the knowledge of God: I speak this to your shame (1 Corinthians 15:34).

> This I say then, Walk in the Spirit, and ye shall not fulfill the lust of the flesh (Galatians 5:16).

> But the fruit of the Spirit is love, joy, peace, longsuf-
> fering, gentleness, goodness, faith, meekness, temper-
> ance: against such there is no law. And they that are
> Christ's have crucified the flesh with the affections
> and lusts (Galatians 5:22-24).

The final generation will be perfect. They will obey God.
They will keep His law, for He has guaranteed to empower
it.

> And the dragon was wroth with the woman, and
> went to make war with the remnant of her seed,
> which keep the commandments of God, and have the
> testimony of Jesus Christ (Revelation 12:17).
>
> Here is the patience of the saints: here are they that
> keep the commandments of God, and the faith of
> Jesus (Revelation 14:12).
>
> And to her was granted that she should be arrayed
> in fine linen, clean and white: for the fine linen is the
> righteousness of saints (Revelation 19:8).
>
> These are they which were not defiled with women;
> for they are virgins. These are they which follow the
> Lamb whithersoever he goeth. These were redeemed
> from among men, being the firstfruits unto God and
> to the Lamb. And in their mouth was found no guile:
> for they are without fault before the throne of God
> (Revelation 14:4, 5).
>
> That he might present it to himself a glorious
> church, not having spot, or wrinkle, or any such thing;
> but that it should be holy and without blemish
> (Ephesians 5:27).
>
> He that is unjust, let him be unjust still: and he
> which is filthy, let him be filthy still: and he that is
> righteous, let him be righteous still: and he that is
> holy, let him be holy still (Revelation 22:11).

These pointed words of Scripture effectively destroy the defeatist theory of the *new theology* which asserts that God does not empower victory over all sin. To accept such error infers one of two assumptions:

>   a) That God will again pollute heaven with sinners.

>   b) He will arbitrarily make saints out of sinners.

Scripture steadfastly denies both these positions.

6. *The new birth takes place at conversion.* The biblical truth is that the new birth and conversion are coincidental. Conversion *is* the new birth experience. In a denominationally published book, *Answers on the Way*, 1977, Dr. Ford said, "Conversion brings to man the Holy Spirit and the spiritual seeds of the new nature." This statement supports the false Evangelical concept that conversion is seed sowing or the insemination of truth; and that the new birth takes place sometime after conversion. This is a radical departure from biblical teaching. If this were true, we would not be in a saving relationship with Jesus between the time of conversion and the rebirth, for Jesus said,

> Verily, verily, I say unto thee, Except a man be born again, he cannot see the kingdom of God (John 3:3).

Yet the Bible declares that those who are born again have Christ's power of victory over sin.

> If ye know that he is righteous, ye know that every one that doeth righteousness is born of him (1 John 2:29).

> We know that whosoever is born of God sinneth not; but he that is begotten of God keepeth himself, and that wicked one toucheth him not (1 John 5:18).

> Knowing this, that our old man is crucified with him, that the body of sin might be destroyed, that

henceforth we should not serve sin. For he that is dead is freed from sin (Romans 6:6, 7).

Seeing ye have purified your souls in obeying the truth through the Spirit unto unfeigned love of the brethren, see that ye love one another with a pure heart fervently: being born again, not of corruptible seed, but of incorruptible, by the word of God, which liveth and abideth for ever (1 Peter 1: 22, 23).

The separation of conversion from the new birth experience is neither logical nor scriptural.

7. *We are in Christ, and Christ is in us.* The Bible teaches that Christians are both in Christ and He in them. Yet some have said that to hold that Christ is in us is a form of Zombiism. The objection offered is that, if Christ is in us, we would have no mind of our own. We would lose our power of choice and decision making. As with many things, this analysis has partial truth. Certainly, if Christ is in us, we will do His will, but there is a vast contrast between the surrender of the will to Satan and the surrender of the will to Christ. When we surrender our will to Satan, he enslaves us and truly we act like Zombies. When we surrender our will to Christ, He frees us. Never does He deprive us of our right to decide. Never will He hold our loyalty against our will. The moment we decide to join the ranks of the enemy, in divine sorrow He permits us to make that choice.

Nothing makes this issue clearer than the parable Christ related concerning the vine and the branches. The question might be asked, "Is the vine in the branch or is the branch in the vine?"

Very obviously, the answer is that both statements are true.

> I am the vine, ye are the branches: *He that abideth in me, and I in him, the same bringeth forth much fruit: for without me ye can do nothing* (John 15:5, emphasis added).

This truth is confirmed in other scriptural passages:

> Hereby know we that we dwell in him, and he in us, because he hath given us of his Spirit (1 John 4:13).

> Whosoever shall confess that Jesus is the Son of God, God dwelleth in him, and he in God (1 John 4:15).

> And he that keepeth his commandments dwelleth in him, and he in him. And hereby we know that he abideth in us, by the Spirit which he hath given us (1 John 3:24).

> Examine yourselves, whether ye be in the faith; prove your own selves. Know ye not your own selves, how that Jesus Christ is in you, except ye be reprobates (2 Corinthians 13:5)?

> I am crucified with Christ: nevertheless I live; yet not I, but Christ liveth in me: and the life which I now live in the flesh I live by the faith of the Son of God, who loved me, and gave himself for me (Galatians 2:20).

> To whom God would make known what is the riches of the glory of this mystery among the Gentiles; which is Christ in you, the hope of glory (Colossians 1:27).

There is no question that sinful, fallen man is born in a state of helplessness. However, the redemptive sacrifice of Jesus Christ not only forgives but restores. God will have a people upon this earth who will reflect His character, who will demonstrate to the world the love and purity of those who have allowed Jesus full and complete reign in their lives. They will provide positive proof that Satan's claim that man cannot obey God's law is false. God's power to transform sinners will be demonstrated before a marveling universe.

Those who are unfamiliar with the *new theology* may find it easy to miss its direction. It is not uncommon for proponents of the *new theology* to uphold the concept of victory over sin. But in reality, they are not upholding Christ's power to provide continual victory. Rather they uphold victory over sin as an unobtainable ideal to which one should strive. *New theology* teachers will frequently make calls for unity. Yet these calls are not focused upon a truth that sanctifies. Indeed, under the cloak of avoiding dissention, they will urge that those doctrines which divide should not be emphasized. This seconds the work of Satan, who has made all distinctive truths controversial. All such calls to unity simply extend the divisions already very much in evidence in God's church.

Those who espouse the *new theology* will often throw out a very strange challenge to those who teach that Christ provides the power to perfect character. Barbed questions are frequently asked by such men. These include, "Are you perfect?" "Do you know anyone who is perfect?" But such matters are not man's responsibility to claim or to judge. It is alone the responsibility of the Lord, the righteous Judge to determine such matters. No perfect individual will claim to be perfect. Man's perfection is always dependent upon Jesus. Often the concepts of perfection are wrongly referred to as legalism but this is a false charge, for they are not predicated upon what man can do but what God has promised to do for His surrendered people.

The biblical concept of perfection does not refer to perfection in the flesh prior to the return of Jesus. Until this mortal puts on immortality and this corruption puts on incorruption, we will possess fallen flesh. This is different from perfection of character. Sister White precisely set forth this distinction when she was combating the holy flesh movement of Indiana.

> "All may now obtain holy hearts, but it is not correct to claim in this life to have holy flesh. . . . And while we cannot claim perfection of the flesh, we may have Christian perfection of the soul (*Selected Messages*, vol. 2, p. 32)."

But God will have a people who will vindicate His name and His character, a people who will be entrusted with the power of the Holy Spirit, who will go forward to give the final invitation of the loud cry to every inhabitant of the world. What a glorious privilege this is for those who will respond to Jesus' call!

7

The Nature of Sin and the New Theology

The correct understanding of the biblical concept of sin is essential to our understanding of salvation. Some of the most significant truths opposed by the *new theology* on this topic are addressed below.

1. *Sin is willful or negligent violation of God's law.* The proponents of the *new theology* present sin as any departure from the infinite will of God and as any weakness or frailty of man. Some are ignorant of the testimony of Scripture. Others totally disregard Scripture in a determined effort to support their erroneous views. Thus anything short of full knowledge is said to be sin. If this were true, then no created beings could live in perfect sinlessness, whether they be angels or redeemed saints, for God alone is omniscient.

Colin once received a letter from a strong protagonist of the *new theology*, asking if he had ever forgotten to mail his wife's letters. The questioner claimed that such forgetfulness was sin. Another leader of the *new theology* once claimed that the crossing of one's legs was sin because it would restrict the optimal flow of blood, and, therefore, was a poor health practice. If this theory were correct, to take such postures would then be to condemn prayer because kneeling on our knees would restrict the flow of blood. Some might see this of little consequence, but it is an essential concept within the tenants of *new theology*. Once the supporters of the *new theology* are convinced that any limitation is sin, then it becomes obvious that no one can ever have victory over sin.

This leads to a sense of carnal security. If man can be saved while persisting in the *sins* of limitation, there is no reason to suspect that he cannot be saved while persisting in other more deliberate sins. Thus the *high* definition of sin, as it is called, is used to deny obedience which God has promised to all those who will serve Him. The so-called *low* definition of sin paradoxically upholds the blessing of obedience to God. The servant of the Lord says there is only one definition of sin:

> Whosoever committeth sin trangresseth also the law: for sin is the transgression of the law (1 John 3:4).

The Lord fully understands the limitation of sinful flesh in which we are all born, but He has promised victory by the renewing of our minds (Romans 12:1, 2). Unequivocally, Inspiration proclaims that God can give us victory over all sin all of the time.

> Let no one say, I cannot remedy my defects of character. If you come to this decision, you will certainly fail of obtaining eternal life (*Christ's Object Lessons*, p. 331).

The very life and ministry of Jesus provided an example for us of victory over sin.

> For even hereunto were ye called: because Christ also suffered for us, leaving us an example, that ye should follow his steps: who did no sin, neither was guile found in his mouth (1 Peter 2:21, 22).

This example of Jesus not only provides the standard of conduct for God's children but, inherent within it, is the divine power to have victory in this life.

2. *God holds no man responsible for sins of ignorance.* The *new theology* falsely claims that God holds man responsible for sins of ignorance. The Bible, on the other hand, establishes the fact that knowledge and understanding are necessary for wrongdoing to be accounted as sin.

The Word of God states that God has compassion upon the ignorant.

> Who can have compassion on the ignorant, and on them that are out of the way; for that he himself also is compassed with infirmity (Hebrews 5:2).

This does not, however, include those who have been negligently ignorant.

> How shall we escape, if we neglect so great salvation; which at the first began to be spoken by the Lord, and was confirmed unto us by them that heard him (Hebrews 2:3).

Those who through no fault of their own do not understand the fullness of God's truth will nevertheless be judged according to their response to the light that they have had.

> For when the Gentiles, which have not the law, do by nature the things contained in the law, these, having not the law, are a law unto themselves: which shew the work of the law written in their hearts, their

conscience also bearing witness, and their thoughts
the mean while accusing or else excusing one another
(Romans 2:14, 15).

In the kingdom of heaven, there will be many who have
been Sabbath breakers, and even idol worshipers, who will
be redeemed. The redeemed heathen have responded to
the leading of the Holy Spirit whom they have never
known and to the Christ of whom they have never learned.

> Even among the heathen are those who have
> cherished the spirit of kindness; before the words of
> life had fallen upon their ears, they have befriended
> the missionaries, even ministering to them at the peril
> of their own lives. Among the heathen are those who
> worship God ignorantly, those to whom the light is
> never brought by human instrumentality, yet they
> will not perish. Though ignorant of the written law of
> God, they have heard His voice speaking to them in
> nature, and have done the things that the law re-
> quired. Their works are evidence that the Holy Spirit
> has touched their hearts, and they are recognized as
> the children of God (*Desire of Ages*, p. 638).

The Bible is replete with statement after statement that
make it clear that God does not hold man responsible for
innocent ignorance.

> Therefore to him that knoweth to do good, and
> doeth it not, to him it is sin (James 4:17).
>
> And the times of this ignorance God winked at; but
> now commandeth all men every where to repent (Acts
> 17:30).

In the ministry of Jesus Christ to the pharisees, He
pointed out that even leaders who were unwittingly ignorant would not have been guilty before God.

Jesus said unto them, If ye were blind, ye should have no sin: but now ye say, We see; therefore your sin remaineth (John 9:41).

If I had not come and spoken unto them, they had not had sin: but now they have no cloak for their sin (John 15:22).

Sin and lawbreaking bring guilt that cries out for forgiveness and pardon.

Then it shall be, because he hath sinned, and is guilty that he shall restore . . . (Leviticus 6:4).

For whosoever shall keep the whole law, and yet offend in one point, he is guilty of all (James 2:10).

Thou shalt not take the name of the Lord thy God in vain; for the Lord will not hold him guiltless that taketh his name in vain (Exodus 20:7).

The sin problem sets a decision before us.

Awake to righteousness, and sin not (1 Corinthians 15:34).

Know ye not, that to whom ye yield yourselves servants to obey, his servants ye are to whom ye obey; whether of sin unto death, or of obedience unto righteousness (Romans 6:16)?

If sin were all the infinite weaknesses of man, then these calls would be unfair and unjust. So also would have been Christ's call to those to whom He ministered.

Neither do I condemn thee: go, and sin no more (John 8:11).

Afterward Jesus findeth him in the temple, and said unto him, Behold, thou art made whole: sin no more, lest a worse thing come unto thee (John 5:14).

The *high* concept of sin leads us to excuse sin, and opens the mind of the believer to a sin-and-live theology. The *low* concept of sin provides the basis by which God perfects His character in His people.

3. *Sin may be overcome now.* One of the trademarks of the *new theology* is the belief that all will continue to sin until Jesus comes. While calls for victory and sanctification are made and growth in righteous conduct is encouraged, those who espouse the *new theology* do not believe that a Spirit-filled man can gain moment by moment victory over sin in this life.

One of the greatest mistakes that Robert Brinsmead made in the 1960s was to indicate that sin would be eradicated by a special act of God at the sealing. This view suggested that victory over sin was not to be gained until the sealing. He had wrongly equated Christ-empowered victory over sin with the blotting out of sin at the final atonement. This error was consistent with his acceptance of the doctrine of original sin. Later Brinsmead simply postponed the timing of the eradication of sin by accepting the Evangelical error that victory over sin does not occur until the Second Coming.

We recall a meeting sponsored by the Greater Sydney Conference in which two ministers pointed out the error of Brinsmead's 1960 view. One, proposing error to correct error, asserted that "Brinsmead is wrong, for we will not have victory until the second coming of Jesus." The other correctly asserted, "Brinsmead is wrong. The Lord wants us to have victory now. We can put away sin now by the power of Christ." Few in that meeting were perceptive enough to foresee that these opposing views would prove to be the whole basis of the division between truth and error in the 1970s.

God has always required perfect obedience of His people. But with that requirement has come the infinite power to have victory. Here are some of the most pertinent biblical statements:

> Forasmuch then as Christ hath suffered for us in the flesh, arm yourselves likewise with the same mind: for he that hath suffered in the flesh hath ceased from sin; that he no longer should live the rest of his time in the flesh to the lusts of men, but to the will of God (1 Peter 4:1, 2).

> Seeing ye have purified your souls in obeying the truth through the Spirit unto unfeigned love of the brethren, see that ye love one another with a pure heart fervently (1 Peter 1:22).

> Knowing this, that our old man is crucified with him, that the body of sin might be destroyed, that henceforth we should not serve sin. For he that is dead is freed from sin (Romans 6:6, 7).

> In whom all the building fitly framed together groweth unto an holy temple in the Lord (Ephesians 2:21).

> That the righteousness of the law might be fulfilled in us, who walk not after the flesh, but after the Spirit (Romans 8:4).

> But thanks be to God, which giveth us the victory through our Lord Jesus Christ (1 Corinthians 15:57).

> Now unto him that is able to keep you from falling, and to present you faultless before the presence of his glory with exceeding joy (Jude 24).

> Teaching us that, denying ungodliness and worldly lusts, we should live soberly, righteously, and godly,

in this present world; looking for that blessed hope, and the glorious appearing of the great God and our Saviour Jesus Christ; who gave himself for us, that he might redeem us from all iniquity, and purify unto himself a peculiar people, zealous of good works (Titus 2:12-14, emphasis added).

Whosoever abideth in him sinneth not: whosoever sinneth hath not seen him, neither known him (1 John 3:6).

We know that whosoever is born of God sinneth not; but he that is begotten of God keepeth himself, and that wicked one toucheth him not (1 John 5:18).

4. *Sin separates from God.* The *new theology* apologists state that we are not separated from God by an occasional sin. Their human reasoning follows the line that God does not play yo-yo with His people. Does a father separate himself from his children because they are disobedient? How much more then would God not separate Himself from man because of occasional sins. The Scripture, it is asserted, is even stronger.

I will not fail thee, nor forsake thee (Joshua 1:5).

Be strong and of a good courage, fear not, nor be afraid of them: for the Lord thy God, he it is that doth go with thee; he will not fail thee, nor forsake thee. And the Lord, he it is that doth go before thee; he will be with thee, he will not fail thee, neither forsake thee: fear not, neither be dismayed (Deuteronomy 31: 6, 8).

Mistakenly, those espousing the *new theology* often suggest that those who believe God's truth declare that God separates Himself because of one sin. This is not true! But it is true that by a single sin *we* separate ourselves from God.

> But your iniquities have separated between you
> and your God, and your sins have hid his face from
> you, that he will not hear (Isaiah 59:2).

When we sin, we separate ourselves from God. For some
unaccountable reason, those who espouse the *new theology*
have not pondered the implications of the fact that one sin
separated Adam and Eve, and, through Adam and Eve,
mankind from the presence of God. They do not recognize
the impact of the revelation that one sin deprived Moses of
entry into the Promised Land. It has been common for the
proponents of the *new theology* to suggest that David was
still in a saving relationship with God when he committed
murder and adultery. But it is obvious that David did not
believe that. He had, at this point, lost his salvation. Thus
he prayed:

> Restore unto me the joy of thy salvation; and
> uphold me with thy free spirit (Psalm 51:12).

Paul emphasizes the truth that we are either in the Spirit
or in the flesh. If we are in the flesh, we cannot be saved;
but, in the Spirit, we have everlasting life.

> For they that are after the flesh do mind the things
> of the flesh; but they that are after the Spirit the things
> of the Spirit. For to be carnally minded is death; but to
> be spiritually minded is life and peace. Because the
> carnal mind is enmity against God: for it is not subject
> to the law of God, neither indeed can be. So then they
> that are in the flesh cannot please God (Romans 8:5-8).

The issue is well-illustrated in the parable of the prodigal
son. The son had certainly disgraced his family, dishonor-
ing his father with his life of wantonness. However, it was

not the father who separated himself from the son. It was the son who separated from the father.

After the few moments of ecstatic pleasure, the boy turned back to his father when he was faced with the awful consequences of his sins. What a beautiful scene is depicted as the boy walks toward his home. He is rehearsing a statement that he hopes will somehow soften the heart of his father. "I am not worthy to be thy son, make me one of thy hired servants."

What a picture of our loving heavenly Father we have in that father! The moment he recognized his son, he ran down the road, not with the sure gait of a young man, but the more awkward gait of a middle-aged man. As he came to his boy, he opened his arms wide and embraced him. The boy starts to splutter out his well-rehearsed speech, but the father was deaf to his words. Taking him into the house, he removed the filthy, tattered garments, washed him, and placed upon him not the robe of a servant but the robe of sonship. When we separate from God by sinning, we are not left hopeless. We have a loving Saviour who has told us:

> My little children, these things write I unto you, that ye sin not. And if any man sin, we have an advocate with the Father, Jesus Christ the righteous (1 John 2:1).

Sadly, the *new theology*, with its concept of sin and repentance, sin again and repentance *ad infinitum*, has not acknowledged the power of God to give us moment by moment, day by day, victory. Such a concept would, indeed, lead to a yo-yo relationship with God. But those who know the love of God, recognize that it is not His desire that we should have such a relationship. Day by day, like Enoch, we can walk with our God in the assurance that He has not only forgiven our sins but that He is able also to keep us from falling. Thus we have the wonderful promise:

> Not rendering evil for evil, or railing for railing: but contrariwise blessing; knowing that ye are thereunto called, that ye should inherit a blessing (1 Peter 3:9).

This page intentionally left blank.

8

The Sanctuary Message and the New Theology, Part 1

The sanctuary message and the interpretation of prophecy were the two major issues upon which the *new theology* was rejected by church leadership at the Glacier View (Colorado) consultation in 1980. The sanctuary message is the most unique doctrine of the Seventh-day Adventist Church. It is neither understood nor taught by any other church. Avid proponents of the *new theology* were eager to take up the arguments which Protestant churches have used against this doctrine. The sanctuary message, they declared, was a face-saving response to the disappointment of 1844. For decades Seventh-day Adventists have faced that kind of assault from the opponents of the Seventh-day Adventist Church. That it surfaced amongst church members, however, was an alarming turn of events. Before the 1970s, there had been a few who had made similar statements from within the church, but never previously had it happened on such a massive scale. Yet Sister White declares the centrality of the sanctuary message to present truth.

> The intercession of Christ in man's behalf in the sanctuary above is as essential to the plan of salvation as was His death upon the cross. By His death He began that work which after His resurrection He ascended to complete in heaven. We must by faith enter within the veil, "whither the forerunner is for us entered" (Hebrews 6:20).

> There the light from the cross of Calvary is reflected. There we may gain a clearer insight into the mysteries of redemption (*Great Controversy*, p. 489).

Let us examine, in the light of Inspiration, the claims of the *new theology* against the truth of the sanctuary message:

1. *The atonement is completed by Christ's high priestly ministry in the heavenly sanctuary.* For many decades now, Evangelicals have assaulted the concept that the atonement is completed by the ministry of Christ in the heavenly sanctuary. They have held that to teach this is to downgrade the sacrificial ministry of Jesus Christ. It is held by Evangelicals and *new theology* supporters alike that the atonement was completed at the cross. In weakness we have often yielded on this point when, indeed, there are compelling biblical reasons to support the Seventh-day Adventist position. Using one isolated statement from Sister White against a large number that clearly state that the atonement of Jesus is completed in the heavenly sanctuary, many have made statements to the effect that "Christ is now ministering the benefits of His atonement in the heavenly sanctuary." But this is an incomplete representation of the doctrine of the atonement. Christ's sacrifice

was, indeed, the central event in the atonement, but so also is His high priestly ministry. The atoning sacrifice of Christ is completed by the ministration of His precious blood in the heavenly sanctuary.

Nowhere in the *Bible* is the atonement better described than in the sixteenth chapter of Leviticus. Here, in the sacrificial type, the word, *atonement,* is mentioned thirteen times. This chapter manifestly declares that the atonement was not limited to the sacrifice, but it also included every single act which took place on the Day of Atonement:

> And Aaron shall offer his bullock of the sin offering, which is for himself, and make an *atonement* for himself, and for his house (Leviticus 16:6, emphasis added).

> But the goat, on which the lot fell to be the scapegoat, shall be presented alive before the Lord, to make an *atonement* with him, and to let him go for a scapegoat into the wilderness (Leviticus 16:10, emphasis added).

> And Aaron shall bring the bullock of the sin offering, which is for himself, and shall make an *atonement* for himself, and for his house, and shall kill the bullock of the sin offering which is for himself (Leviticus 16:11, emphasis added).

> And he shall make an *atonement* for the holy place, because of the uncleanness of the children of Israel, and because of their transgressions in all their sins: and so shall he do for the tabernacle of the congregation, that remaineth among them in the midst of their uncleanness (Leviticus 16:16, emphasis added).

> And there shall be no man in the tabernacle of the congregation when he goeth in to make an *atonement* in the holy place, until he come out, and have made

an *atonement* for himself, and for his household, and for all the congregation of Israel (Leviticus 16:17, emphasis added).

And he shall wash his flesh with water in the holy place, and put on his garments, and come forth, and offer his burnt offering, and the burnt offering of the people, and make an *atonement* for himself, and for the people (Leviticus 16:24, emphasis added).

For on that day shall the priest make an *atonement* for you, to cleanse you, that ye may be clean from all your sins before the Lord (Leviticus 16:30, emphasis added).

And the priest, whom he shall anoint, and whom he shall consecrate to minister in the priest's office in his father's stead, shall make the *atonement*, and shall put on the linen clothes, even the holy garments (Leviticus 16:32, emphasis added).

And he shall make an *atonement* for the holy sanctuary, and he shall make an *atonement* for the tabernacle of the congregation, and for the altar, and he shall make an *atonement* for the priests, and for all the people of the congregation (Leviticus 16:33, emphasis added).

And this shall be an everlasting statute unto you, to make an *atonement* for the children of Israel for all their sins once a year. And he did as the Lord commanded Moses (Leviticus 16:34, emphasis added).

Thus Leviticus, chapter 16 demonstrates that the atonement included the sacrifice of the bullocks for the high priest and his family. It included the sacrifice of the Lord's goat. It included the disposition of the scapegoat. It included the ministry of the blood on and before the mercy seat of the heavenly sanctuary. To define the atonement apart from the high priestly ministry of Jesus is to deny the testimony of Scripture. This in no wise depreciates the cross and the perfect and completed sacrificial atonement made by Christ. It rather opens to our understanding the unity between Christ's ministry as both our Sacrifice and our heavenly High Priest. Every act of Christ demonstrates the infinite love of God for the inhabitants of this sinful race.

So complete is Christ's atonement in the heavenly sanctuary that the sins of ignorance of the righteous dead are also blotted out in the investigative judgment.

> This atonement is made for the righteous dead as well as for the righteous living. It includes all who died trusting in Christ, but who, not having received the light upon God's commandments, had sinned ignorantly in transgressing its precepts (*Early Writings*, p. 254).

Some take hold of Christ's words just immediately proceeding His death, "It is finished" (John 19:30), and then assume that Christ was declaring that His atonement was finished. Certainly the sacrifice was completed. Certainly the reconciliation of man was also completed. Certainly, by His death, He had drawn all men unto Him. Certainly His battle with Satan was completed. It is, however, an unwarranted assumption to say that His atonement was finished, for such a conclusion disputes the words of Scripture. Leviticus 16, in type, clarifies the fact that Christ could not have been referring to His atonement is His declaration that *"It is finished!"* Rather than diminishing the focus of the cross, the beautiful sanctuary message sees the cross as the centerpiece of the sanctuary message.

2. *Christ began His Most Holy Place ministry in 1844.* It will be recalled that a restudy of the Scripture immediately after the disappointment of 1844 led to a fuller understanding of the message of Daniel 8:14.

> And he said unto me, Unto two thousand and three hundred days; then shall the sanctuary be cleansed (Daniel 8:14).

Whereas the Millerites had believed that the cleansing of the sanctuary referred to the cleansing of the earth by fire at the end of the world, the pioneers of the Seventh-day Adventist Church early realized that this was not a reference to the destruction of the earth but to the cleansing of the heavenly sanctuary by Jesus our heavenly High Priest. This is vividly described in both the Old and New Testament:

> And let them make me a sanctuary; that I may dwell among them. According to all that I shew thee, after the pattern of the tabernacle, and the pattern of all the instruments thereof, even so shall ye make it (Exodus 25:8, 9).

> Now of the things which we have spoken this is the sum: We have such an high priest, who is set on the right hand of the throne of the Majesty in the heavens; a minister of the sanctuary, and of the true tabernacle, which the Lord pitched, and not man. For every high priest is ordained to offer gifts and sacrifices: wherefore it is of necessity that this man have somewhat also to offer. For if he were on earth, he should not be a priest, seeing that there are priests that offer gifts according to the law: who serve unto the example and shadow of heavenly things, as Moses was admonished of God when he was about to make the tabernacle: for, See, saith he, that thou make all things

according to the pattern shewed to thee in the mount (Hebrews 8:1-5).

A careful study of the types of the Old Testament reveal that there were two phases of the ministry of the high priest. The daily ministry dealt with the forgiveness of sins. The yearly ministry on the Day of Atonement dealt with the blotting out of sin. It is evident that the blotting out of sins in the antitype takes place right at the end of time when the Holy Spirit is poured out upon men:

> Repent ye therefore, and be converted, that your sins may be blotted out, when the times of refreshing shall come from the presence of the Lord (Acts 3:19).

As the sins of the saints are blotted from the books of heaven, so they are blotted from their memory.

> As in the final atonement the sins of the truly penitent are to be blotted from the records of heaven, no more to be remembered or come into mind, so in the type they were borne away into the wilderness, forever separated from the congregation (*Patriarchs and Prophets*, p. 358).

> The righteous will not cease their earnest agonizing cries for deliverance. They cannot bring to mind any particular sins, but in their whole life they can see but little good. Their sins had gone beforehand to judgment, and pardon had been written. Their sins had been borne away into the land of forgetfulness, and they could not bring them to remembrance (*Spiritual Gifts*, vol. 3, p. 135).

> But while they have a deep sense of their unworthiness, they have no concealed wrongs to reveal. Their sins have gone beforehand to judgment and have been blotted out, and they cannot bring them to remembrance (*Great Controversy*, p. 620).

3. *The end of the world began at the end of medieval Roman Catholic dominance.* Many believers in the *new theology* argue that the end of the world commenced in apostolic time. They quote such texts as:

> For then must he often have suffered since the foundation of the world: but now once in the end of the world hath he appeared to put away sin by the sacrifice of himself (Hebrews 9:26).

> God, who at sundry times and in divers manners spake in time past unto the fathers by the prophets, hath in these last days spoken unto us by his Son, whom he hath appointed heir of all things, by whom also he made the worlds (Hebrews 1:1, 2).

> Who verily was foreordained before the foundation of the world, but was manifest in these last times for you (1 Peter 1:20).

> Little children, it is the last time: and as ye have heard that antichrist shall come, even now are there many antichrists; whereby we know that it is the last time (1 John 2:18).

Yet such individuals tend to ignore other texts which look to the end of time somewhere in the future.

> How that they told you there should be mockers in the last time, who should walk after their own ungodly lusts (Jude 18).

> This know also, that in the last days perilous times shall come (2 Timothy 3:1).

> Your gold and silver is cankered; and the rust of them shall be a witness against you, and shall eat your flesh as it were fire: Ye have heaped treasure together for the last days (James 5:3).

Who are kept by the power of God through faith unto salvation ready to be revealed in the last time (1 Peter 1:5).

Knowing this first, that there shall come in the last days scoffers, walking after their own lusts (2 Peter 3:3).

The reconciliation of these two apparently opposing sets of texts is not difficult. It will be remembered that in the dialogue of Christ with His disciples, they had asked,

Tell us, when shall these things be [the destruction of the temple in Jerusalem]? and what shall be the sign of thy coming, and of the end of the world (Matthew 24:3, brackets added)?

With this dual emphasis, it was appropriate for the disciples to refer to the days in which they lived as the latter days. It was also appropriate for them to look to the future for the end of the world. However, by applying the term "the latter days" exclusively to the apostolic period, the *new theology* claims that the time of the end began in A.D. 31. Therefore they conclude that Christ began His Second Apartment ministry at that time.

This erroneous conclusion is heavily reenforced by a misunderstanding of other passages in Scripture which state that upon His ascension, Christ was seated on the right hand of His Father:

But this man, after he had offered one sacrifice for sins for ever, *sat down on the right hand of God* (Hebrews 10:12, emphasis added).

Looking unto Jesus the author and finisher of our faith; who for the joy that was set before him endured the cross, despising the shame, and is *set down at the right hand of the throne of God* (Hebrews 12:2, emphasis added).

Therefore *being by the right hand of God* exalted, and having received of the Father the promise of the Holy Ghost, he hath shed forth this, which ye now see and hear (Acts 2:33, emphasis added).

Who being the brightness of his glory, and the express image of his person, and upholding all things by the word of his power, when he had by himself purged our sins, *sat down on the right hand of the Majesty on high* (Hebrews 1:3, emphasis added).

So then after the Lord had spoken unto them, he was received up into heaven, and *sat on the right hand of God* (Mark 16:19, emphasis added).

This act of Christ fulfilled the prophecy of David:

The Lord said unto my Lord, Sit thou at my right hand, until I make thine enemies thy footstool (Psalm 110:1).

In an incredibly naive approach to Scripture, many believers in the *new theology* claim that these texts prove that Christ is sitting next to the Father. It would be difficult to imagine a juxtaposition like this for 2,000 years. With this kind of concept in mind, it has been argued that where God is must be the Most Holy Place in the universe. Therefore Christ must have gone immediately into the Most Holy Place. Thus human interpretation is cited as if it carried the weight of biblical certainty.

It is important for us to realize that the Hebrew language is one of the most concrete languages in the world. It frequently deals with abstract concepts in concrete terms. While the writers of the New Testament were writing in Greek, they were writing with the mind-set of the Hebrew.

Indeed, even in the English language, this use of the concrete is understood. If someone states "He is my right-hand man," we know what is meant. This man is the closest to him and the one upon whom he primarily depends.

When May Day is celebrated in Moscow, the Soviet watchers are always interested to discover who is closest to the general secretary. The change in positions indicate a change in authority. Thus in everyday life the term, *right-hand man*, has a meaning beyond that of proximity. It relates to position and authority.

But the Bible, itself, elucidates the meaning of this idiom. The mother of Zebedee's children came to the Lord, to ask a favor.

> And he said unto her, What wilt thou? She saith unto him, Grant that these my two sons may sit, the one on thy right hand, and the other on the left in thy kingdom (Matthew 20:21).

Simply she was stating, *I desire one of my sons to be first in your kingdom, after you, and the other to be second.* The constant references to Christ on the right hand of the Father have nothing to do with a physical seating arrangement, rather it deals with authority and relationship. It is a wonderful joy to understand that no one in the universe stands between Christ and His Father. Our heavenly High Priest and Mediator is one with the Father. The statement of the prophet Daniel, couched in prophetic language, is that at the end of the 2300 days (that is, 1844) Christ began His day of atonement, Second Apartment ministry for mankind.

Some have argued that Christ's first apartment ministry took place during the Old Testament dispensation, and that the New Testament dispensation is the dispensation of the Second Apartment ministry. But how could this be? The Scripture explains that

> Without the shedding of blood is no remission (Hebrews 9:22).

Before the sacrifice of Christ, there was no atoning blood to minister. On His ascension to heaven, Christ began His ministry of forgiveness, pardon, and justification. It is rather difficult to understand the thinking of those who emphasize a justification alone gospel, and further claim that the sacrifice of Christ alone was required for our justification. For, despite these presuppositions, many illogically hold that before the sacrifice of Jesus, Christ's work of justification would have been completed. This is an explanation which defies credibility.

In the typical Day of Atonement, all Israelites solemnly afflicted their souls before coming before the Lord.

> And this shall be a statute for ever unto you: that in the seventh month, on the tenth day of the month, ye shall afflict your souls, and do no work at all, whether it be one of your own country, or a stranger that sojourneth among you (Leviticus 16:29).

So there is to be a special work of putting away of sin in the lives of the believers during Christ's ministry in the Second Apartment of the heavenly sanctuary.

> While the investigative judgment is going forward in heaven, while the sins of penitent believers are being removed from the sanctuary, there is to be a special work of purification, of putting away of sin,

among God's people upon earth (*Great Controversy*, p. 425).

This is a solemn time for God's faithful children.

4. *The judgment of the living takes place before the close of human probation.* Hard-core proponents of the *new theology* have long declared that the investigative judgment is a myth. They have claimed that there is no biblical support for it. They claim that the judgment of the living takes place at the second coming of Jesus. But, of all the judgments of God, none is more fully enshrined in Scripture than the investigative judgment. The judgment in Eden is clarified in only one text.

> Therefore as by the offence of one judgment came upon all men to condemnation; even so by the righteousness of one the free gift came upon all men unto justification of life (Romans 5:18).

The judgment of the cross is described only by John.

> Now is the judgment of this world: now shall the prince of this world be cast out. And I, if I be lifted up from the earth, will draw all men unto me (John 12:31, 32).

The judgment by the saints after their redemption is mentioned infrequently in the Bible:

> And I saw thrones, and they sat upon them, and judgment was given unto them: and I saw the souls of them that were beheaded for the witness of Jesus and for the word of God, and which had not worshipped the beast, neither his image, neither had received his mark upon their foreheads, or in their hands; and they lived and reigned with Christ a thousand years (Revelation 20:4).

> Do ye not know that the saints shall judge the world? . . . Know ye not that we shall judge angels (1 Corinthians 6:2, 3)?

The executive judgment of God's destruction is mentioned only a few times:

> And the angels which kept not their first estate, but left their own habitation, he hath reserved in everlasting chains under darkness unto the judgment of the great day (Jude 6).

> To execute judgment upon all, and to convince all that are ungodly among them of all their ungodly deeds which they have ungodly committed, and of all their hard speeches which ungodly sinners have spoken against him (Jude 15).

> For the Lord knoweth the way of the righteous: but the way of the ungodly shall perish (]Psalm 1:6).

> For if God spared not the angels that sinned, but cast them down to hell, and delivered them into chains of darkness, to be reserved unto judgment . . . The Lord knoweth how to deliver the godly out of temptations, and to reserve the unjust unto the day of judgment to be punished (2 Peter 2:4, 9).

Much more extensive treatment is given in the Scriptures to the end-time judgment, known to Seventh-day Adventists as the investigative judgment. Firstly, we know that this judgment comes after the rise of the little horn (Daniel 7:8). It is located in time even more specifically in the later portion of Daniel, chapter 7. Indeed, after the end of the 1260 years of papal authority in 1798 and before the return of Jesus, this judgment takes place:

> And he shall speak great words against the most High, and shall wear out the saints of the most High, and think to change times and laws: and they shall be

given into his hand until a time and times and the dividing of time. But the judgment shall sit, and they shall take away his dominion, to consume and to destroy it unto the end. And the kingdom and dominion, and the greatness of the kingdom under the whole heaven, shall be given to the people of the saints of the most High, whose kingdom is an everlasting kingdom, and all dominions shall serve and obey him (Daniel 7:25-27).

In each description of this judgment, it is shown to come before the end of the world (Daniel 7:14, Daniel 7:27). Therefore, we can be certain that this judgment transpires just prior to the end of time and the establishment of the kingdom of God. This is consistent with the first angel's message of Revelation:

And I saw another angel fly in the midst of heaven, having the everlasting gospel to preach unto them that dwell on the earth, and to every nation, and kindred, and tongue, and people. Saying with a loud voice, Fear God, and give glory to him; for the hour of his judgment is come: and worship him that made heaven, and earth, and the sea, and the fountains of waters (Revelation 14:6,7).

And I looked, and behold a white cloud, and upon the cloud one sat like unto the Son of man, having on his head a golden crown, and in his hand a sharp sickle (Revelation 14:14).

5. *The judgment of Daniel, chapter 7, is against the little horn and for the saints.* Some have said that the judgment of Daniel 7 is not a judgment upon the saints. These assert that it is a judgment upon the little horn. Such people cite the following texts in support of their position:

> I beheld then because of the voice of the great words which the horn spake: I beheld even till the beast was slain, and his body destroyed, and given to the burning flame. . . . But the judgment shall sit, and they shall take away his dominion, to consume and to destroy it unto the end (Daniel 7:11, 26).

Seventh-day Adventists have *not* said that the investigative judgment is for the saints alone. We have stated that all who profess to be God's people are judged at this time. This was the testimony of the type. Of course the little horn, representing the great apostate papal power of the ages, has made great boasts that it is the authentic representative of God on earth.

Therefore those who have given allegiance to the papacy also come into judgment. In this judgment, God is making a final declaration *against* the apostate little horn and its followers, and *in favor* of His people. Indeed, Daniel specifically states this fact. We have the clearest declaration that the judgment is *for* God's people.

> And at that time shall Michael stand up, the great prince which standeth for the children of thy people: and there shall be a time of trouble, such as never was since there was a nation even to that same time: and at that time thy people shall be delivered, every one that shall be found written in the book (Daniel 12:1).

Earlier in his prophetic work, Daniel had stated that the judgment includes God's people in addition to the little horn power.

> Until the Ancient of days came, and judgment was given to the saints [modern translations, "given in favor of the saints"] of the most High; and the time

came that the saints possessed the kingdom (Daniel 7:22).

6. *God has a divine purpose in the investigative judgment.* There are others who argue that God does not need an investigative judgment. He has known from eternity who will be saved. This is true, but the created beings of the universe are not omniscient; and, in the determined purposes of God to secure the universe for eternity, the angels and other unfallen beings have the opportunity to review the records. In this investigative judgment, unfallen beings verify God's perfect justice, and can also be assured that no sinner will again pollute the universe. They also see that no individual worthy of salvation has been excluded from God's kingdom.

> A fiery stream issued and came forth from before him: thousand thousands ministered unto him, and ten thousand times ten thousand stood before him: the judgment was set, and the books were opened (Daniel 7:10).

> And I beheld, and I heard the voice of many angels round about the throne and the beasts and the elders: and the number of them was ten thousand times ten thousand, and thousands of thousands (Revelation 5:11).

The investigative judgment is one of the most beautiful doctrines of the Seventh-day Adventist Church. Some have been intimidated by it; and, certainly, it is a fearful time for the wicked. But to the one who has responded to the matchless claims of Jesus upon his life and service, it is the time when his Lord, his Saviour, stands up for him in the judgment. No one need stand alone. The great sanctuary message offers wonderful hope for every believer.

When the sanctuary is cleansed, Christ has made the final and full atonement for His people.

9

The Sanctuary Message and the New Theology, Part 2

Further exploration of the sanctuary doctrine of the *new theology* reveals the tragic poverty of its biblical foundations. Proponents deny every biblical principle of this great message.

1. *There is a literal heavenly sanctuary.* As time has passed, the rejection of the sanctuary message by those wedded to the *new theology* has become more apparent. Colin will never forget the first indications of this. The year was 1962. He was dialoging with Dr. Desmond Ford. The doctrine of the sanctuary message was discussed, and Colin indicated that he believed in a literal sanctuary in heaven. Dr. Ford, in surprise, replied, "You don't believe in a literal sanctuary in heaven, do you?" Colin responded, "I most certainly do." In response to this affirmation, Dr. Ford offered a diversionary question. "Which is more important, the ministry or the geography?" This question has been asked many times since.

Colin, while quite surprised at Dr. Ford's position, in no wise envisaged the way this *small* departure from truth was to eventually impact upon Dr. Ford's whole sanctuary theology. At this point, Dr. Ford strongly affirmed his belief in the heavenly sanctuary ministry of Jesus Christ and the truths related to the events of 1844.[1] From this experience, we learned more fully than ever that one departure from truth begins a journey, the end of which leads to rejection of all truth. It is never safe to reject any portion of God's Word.

Indisputably, the Scriptures confirm the truth that there is a real sanctuary in heaven. Some have asked questions such as, "How can you put Christ into a box?" The implication of such a question is that it is impossible to confine God in a little sanctuary or temple. We agree God cannot be contained, not even in a gigantic sanctuary. It is important, however, to recognize the significant differences between the heavenly sanctuary and the earthly. There is no question that the heavenly sanctuary is not made with the same materials as was the earthly sanctuary. Animal skins which were used in the construction of the tabernacle on earth most certainly have no place in the heavenly counterpart. It is also essential to recognize that the heavenly sanctuary is of vast proportions. So vast indeed is it, that billions of angels serve there.

> A fiery stream issued and came forth from before him: thousand thousands ministered unto him, and ten thousand times ten thousand stood before him: the judgment was set, and the books were opened (Daniel 7:10).

> And I beheld, and I heard the voice of many angels round about the throne and the beasts and the elders: and the number of them was ten thousand times ten thousand, and thousands of thousands (Revelation 5:11).

Yet, the earthly sanctuary was most assuredly a pattern of that heavenly sanctuary.

> According to all that I shew thee, after the pattern of the tabernacle, and the pattern of all the instruments thereof, even so shall ye make it (Exodus 25:9).

> A minister of the sanctuary, and of the true tabernacle, which the Lord pitched, and not man. For every high priest is ordained to offer gifts and sacrifices: wherefore it is of necessity that this man have somewhat also to offer. . . . Who serve unto the example and shadow of *heavenly* things, as Moses was admonished of God when he was about to make the tabernacle: for, See, saith he, that thou make all things according to the pattern shewed to thee in the mount (Hebrews 8:2, 3, 5, emphasis added).

> And the temple of God was opened in heaven, and there was seen in his temple the ark of his testament (Revelation 11:19).

These texts leave not a shadow of doubt that there is a real and actual sanctuary in heaven. The problem is that once we move one step away from revealed scriptural truth we are in Satan's territory. While Colin did not foresee it, Dr. Ford's denial of the reality of the heavenly sanctuary was the basis upon which today we have the denial of the ministry as well as the geography of the heavenly sanctuary.

Dr. Ford sought to support his contention from the book of Hebrews:

> For Christ is not entered into the holy places made with hands, which are the figures of the true; but into heaven itself, now to appear in the presence of God for us (Hebrews 9:24).

However, it will be seen that in no wise does this verse deny the existence of a heavenly sanctuary. Indeed, Hebrews 9:23 confirms its reality.

> It was therefore necessary that the patterns of things in the *heavens* should be purified with these; but the *heavenly* things themselves with better sacrifices than these (Hebrews 9:23, emphasis added).

Paul here emphasizes the fact that Christ did not enter a man-made sanctuary, as was the one on earth, but that His ministry is now being fulfilled in the sanctuary created by God.

2. *Hebrews 9 supports the Seventh-day Adventist sanctuary concepts.*[2] There is no evidence that Christ entered the Most Holy Place upon His ascension. One of the key errors of the *new theology* is the contention that immediately upon His ascension Christ began His Most Holy Place ministry in heaven. This is almost exclusively predicated upon Paul's statement in Hebrews 9:12. In the King James Version of Scripture it reads as follows:

> Neither by the blood of goats and calves, but by his own blood he entered in once into the holy place, having obtained eternal redemption for us (Hebrews 9:12).

However, in some modern translations, such as the New International Version and the New King James Version, *holy place* is mistranslated *Most Holy Place*.

> He did not enter by means of the blood of goats and calves; but he entered the Most Holy Place once for all by his own blood, having obtained eternal redemption (Hebrews 9:12, NIV).

The question then remains, "Is the translation, *Most Holy Place*, an accurate translation of the Greek?" The answer is a resounding *no*.

The key to this problem lies in the understanding of the Greek word, *ta hagia*, and its grammatical variations. Few words in the Greek have caused more difficulties to Bible students than this word. The initial problem faced is to determine whether *ta hagia* is singular or plural in number. Since the spelling in ancient Greek is identical for both, this makes it difficult to definitely know Paul's intention. It is true that later manuscript copyists placed emphasis marks on this Greek word in order to distinguish between the singular and plural forms. In these later manuscripts, scholars have indicated that *ta hagia*, as used by Paul, was plural. However, this is hardly absolute proof. Thus the word may literally be interpreted either *holy place* or *holy places*, depending upon whether Paul intended the singular or the plural. If he meant holy places, that of course, embraced the sanctuary as a whole.

Many Bibles, including the King James Version, have translated this word variously, *sanctuary, holy place, Most Holy Place*, and by other words which are synonyms of these three terms. However, in Hebrews 9:12, there is no logical nor contextual basis to translate *ta hagia* as *Most Holy Place*. In the only passage in the book of Hebrews in which Paul definitely refers to the Most Holy Place, he does not use the form, *ta hagia*, but *hagia, hagion* (literally, the Holy of the Holiest).

> And after the second veil, the tabernacle which is called the *Holiest of all* (Hebrews 9:3, emphasis added).

Thus when Paul wanted to specify the Most Holy Place, he used this compound term, *hagia, hagion*. Therefore it would be logical that if ever Paul was again referring to the Most Holy Place, he would have used the same compound words; but he never does. The only valid translations of *ta hagia* in Hebrews would be sanctuary or holy place. Many translations consistently use sanctuary. Among these are *The New English Bible* and *The Jerusalem Bible*.

If the proponents of the *new theology* were right in their claim that Christ began His ministry in the Most Holy Place in A.D. 31, then our understanding of the significance of the date, 1844, would be a myth; and the Seventh-day Adventist Church would have no reason for its existence. But Hebrews 9:12, when correctly translated, provides no basis whatsoever for the claims put forth in their theory. This passage is not even addressing the matter of Christ's ministry in the Most Holy Place. It is rather addressing the overall ministry of the High Priest in heaven, comparing His ministry with that of the high priest on earth.

3. *The heavenly sanctuary is polluted by man's sins.* Some proponents of the *new theology* have strongly objected to the concept that has been taught by the Seventh-day Adventist Church, which asserts that the heavenly sanctuary is polluted by man's sins. In this argument, they ask, "How it can be that a perfect heaven can be polluted by the sins of humanity?" In so questioning, they have sought to deny the reality of the investigative judgment and the cleansing of the heavenly sanctuary as indicated in a study of Daniel 8:14. This is a surprising argument, one indicating little depth of scriptural understanding. Long before there was sin on this

planet, or, indeed, this planet was created, there was pollution by sin in heaven. When Lucifer rebelled against God, he and ultimately a third of the angels were cast out because they had polluted heaven by their sins. In a very real sense, the entire universe has been polluted by sin. This has necessitated a plan of redemption of cosmic proportions.

Referring now to the heavenly sanctuary, Paul confirms that there is pollution in the heavenly sanctuary as a result of man's sin:

> It was therefore necessary that the patterns of things in the heavens should be purified with these; but the heavenly things themselves with better sacrifices than these (Hebrews 9:23).

The powerful message of the cleansing of the heavenly sanctuary, as understood by Seventh-day Adventists, is, indeed, consistent with biblical teachings.

4. *Daniel 8:14 is properly linked with Leviticus 16: 30.* [3] The teachers of *new theology* have long challenged the linking of Leviticus 16:30 with Daniel 8:14. They have argued, in a manner persuasive to many superficial students of the Word, that the pioneers of the Seventh-day Adventist message were rather naive theologically. Thus these pioneers, they assert, failed to realize that the word translated *cleansed* in Daniel 8:14 was the Hebrew word, *nisdaq*, whereas the Hebrew word used for *cleanse* in Leviticus 16:30 was *taher*. Obviously these are two entirely different words. Further, it has been pointed out that *nisdaq* has more commonly been translated as *restored, justified,* or *reconsecrated* by modern translators. Therefore, it is argued, there is no justification for linking Daniel

8:14 with Leviticus 16:30. But this argument cannot stand up in the light of close investigation.

We must not forget that 800 or 900 years transpired between the authoring of the books of Leviticus and Daniel. One was written in the Sinai desert and the other in Babylon. We do not question the reasonableness of the modern translations of *nisdaq*. As noted, some translations have used words other than cleansed or purified. Nevertheless, it is a significant observation that the rabbis who translated the Septuagint used the Greek word for *cleansed* in their translation, thus indicating their understanding of the meaning of *nisdaq*. The scholarship of these men cannot be ignored lightly.

Some proponents of the *new theology* have defended their position by suggesting that the translators of the Septuagint were influenced by the desecration of the Jewish Temple by Antiochus Epiphanes in the second century B.C., but there is no evidence to validate this conclusion. This is pure speculation, conveniently proposed to support a false position. Unquestionably, the Hebrew scholars of the second century B.C. certainly equated *nisdaq* with *cleansed.*

An understanding of Hebrew poetry is most helpful in elucidating the use of *nisdaq* in Daniel 8:14. While the word *nisdaq* is not used elsewhere in Scripture, it is a derivative from the root word, *sadaq*, which occurs quite a number of times in the Old Testament. It is fascinating to discover that *taher* is used a number of times in poetic parallelism with *sadaq*. Hebrew poetic structure repeats the same thought in different words. This form of parallelism is the central element of Hebrew poetry. Examples of this poetic form are:

Blessed is he whose transgression is forgiven, whose sin is covered (Psalm 32:1).

I acknowledged my sin unto thee, and my iniquity have I not hid (Psalm 32:5).

I will instruct thee and teach thee in the way which thou shalt go: I will guide thee with mine eye (Psalm 32:8).

I will bless the Lord at all times: his praise shall continually be in my mouth (Psalm 34:1).

Oh magnify the Lord with me, and let us exalt His name together (Psalm 34:3).

Now none of these verses use *sadaq* or *taher*. But four passages of poetry do. In each instance the Hebrew word from which the English word is translated, is indicated in parenthesis:

Shall mortal man be more just [sadaq] than God? shall a man be more pure [taher] than his maker (Job 4:17)?

The righteous [sadaq] also shall hold on his way, and he that hath clean [taher] hands shall be stronger and stronger (Job 17:9).

The fear of the Lord is clean [taher], enduring forever: the judgments of the Lord are true and righteous [sadaq] altogether (Psalm 19:9).

All things come alike to all: there is one event to the righteous [sadaq], and to the wicked; to the good and to the clean [taher], and to the unclean (Ecclesiastes 9:2).

So the fact that the word *nisdag* was used by Daniel and *taher* by Moses to express a similar meaning should not surprise us.

The pioneers of the Seventh-day Adventist Church may have been theologically naive, but they certainly were not biblically naive. The test of investigation fully supports the linking of the cleansing of the Day of Atonement in the typical services with the antitypical cleansing of the heavenly sanctuary by Jesus Christ as outlined by Daniel.

5. *The year 1844 has great biblical significance.* Much doubt has been cast by *new theology* proponents upon the validity of the 2300-day prophecy. Some question the day-year principle, though this was so clearly established in prophetic understanding long before the emergence of the Seventh-day Adventist Church. So we do not here intend to go into this issue. Secondly, some question the date, 457 B.C., as the commencement of the 2300-day prophecy. But, in the light of Scripture, there cannot be another decree other than the accumulative decree of Darius, Cyrus, and Artaxerxes. The prophet Ezra treats them as a single decree:

> And the elders of the Jews builded, and they prospered through the prophesying of Haggai the prophet and Zachariah the son of Iddo. And they builded, and finished it, according to the commandment of the God of Israel, and according to the commandment of Cyrus, and Darius, and Artaxerxes king of Persia (Ezra 6:14).

There is no question that the decree of Artaxerxes was made in 457 B.C. This is the seventh year of the reign of King Artaxerxes, an established historical date. The 2300-day prophecy assuredly finds its fulfillment in the year 1844.

6. *The 2300 evenings and mornings of Daniel 8:14 cannot be 2300 sacrifices.* There is another major issue that has been raised by some. They believe that it is impossible to translate Daniel 8:14 as 2300 days. Literally the Hebrew states, "2300 evenings and mornings." These opponents of truth have

stated that the 2300 evenings and mornings relate to the sacrifices which were offered twice daily in the Jewish sanctuary. From this fact they conclude that the expression, *2300 evenings and mornings,* refers to a period of half the 2300 days or 1150 days. Indeed, there have been a few translations that have translated these evenings and mornings as 1150 days. However the issue is very simple. Days in Scripture are referred to as *evenings and mornings:*

> And God saw the light, that it was good: and God divided the light from the darkness. . . . And the evening and the morning were the first day (Genesis 1:4).

Whenever the daily sacrifices are referred to, they are called the *morning and evening* sacrifices:

> Behold, I build an house to the name of the Lord my God, to dedicate it to him, and to burn before him sweet incense, and for the continual shewbread, and for the burnt offerings *morning and evening* (2 Chronicles 2:4, emphasis added).

> To offer burnt offerings unto the Lord upon the altar of the burnt offering continually *morning and evening,* and to do according to all that is written in the law of the Lord, which he commanded Israel (1 Chronicles 16:40, emphasis added).

> He appointed also the king's portion of his substance for the burnt offerings, to wit, for the *morning and evening* burnt offerings, and the burnt offerings for the sabbaths, and for the new moons, and for the set feasts, as it is written in the law of the Lord (2 Chronicles 31:3, emphasis added).

> And they set the altar upon his bases; for fear was upon them because of the people of those countries: and they offered burnt offerings thereon unto the Lord, even

burnt offerings *morning and evening* (Ezra 3:3, emphasis added).

Thus the 2300 evenings and mornings of Daniel 8:14 must properly be translated 2300 days. In recent years, a Seventh-day Adventist pastor successfully used this agreement to convince Italian biblical scholars who were preparing a modern translation of the Bible.

7. *The cross with the sanctuary ministry of Christ is the center of our hope.* Some opponents claim that Seventh-day Adventists put the sanctuary message ahead of Christ. Others have said that the sanctuary message diminished the centrality to man's salvation of the cross of Christ. Neither of these arguments is biblical. Christ is the center of the sanctuary message. He is our heavenly High Priest. He is our Advocate, our Intercessor, our Mediator, and our Judge.

Properly understood and presented, the centrality of Jesus and the salvation of the cross are beautifully enhanced and illuminated by the sanctuary message. Certainly the sanctuary message does not minimize the focal point of the cross. The sacrifice is central to the sanctuary message. Christ, as our Sacrifice and High Priest, brings together in one great unity His salvation acts for us.

It may be true that at times, unwittingly, Seventh-day Adventists have been so burdened to present this crucial sanctuary message that they have not presented it in the context of the cross of Calvary or the centrality of Jesus Christ. It is impossible for this end-time message to be presented adequately or winningly without uplifting our blessed Saviour. The glorious concept that Christ is everything to us is central to an understanding of this sanctuary message.

Endnotes

[1] On October 27, 1979, Dr. Ford, in an address to the Forum at Pacific Union College, asserted that he had not believed the sanctuary message for 30 years.

[2] For a fuller discussion of this topic, see *Adventism Unveiled* (Appendicies A, B, & C) by the same authors, published by Hartland Publications.

[3] For a fuller discussion of this topic, see *Adventism Unveiled* by the same authors, published by Hartland Publications.

This page intentionally left blank.

10

Prophetic Interpretation and the New Theology

Despite insistence that they are the authentic heirs of Reformation theology, those espousing the *new theology* have deviated dramatically from the Reformers in their interpretation of prophecy. However, they have not deviated from Catholic theology; and, whereas, their salvation principles are etched deeply in Augustinian error, in prophetic interpretation, they have followed the Catholic Jesuit interpretation first set forth at the time of the Counter-Reformation.

At the time of the Reformation, all major Reformers, including Wycliffe, Huss, Jerome, Luther, Zwingli, Calvin, Knox, and Malanchthon, identified the papacy as the antichrist, the man of sin, and the son of perdition. This so alarmed the papacy that one of the greatest endeavors of the Council of Trent (1545-1563) was directed to prophetic interpretation in a vain effort to turn men's eyes away from the identification of the papacy as the antichrist. In the end, this work was entrusted to the new order of intelligencia, the Jesuits.

Eventually two young Jesuit scholars advanced *solutions* to the papal dilemma. Taking hold of the erroneous interpretation of Daniel, chapters 8-12, suggested by the Maccabees in the second century B.C., Louis de Alcasar identified the rather obscure Selucid king, Antiochus Epiphanes, as the antichrist. It is true that Antiochus Epiphanes had conquered Judah for a brief period of time. He had desecrated the Temple by offering a pig as a sacrifice in the Most Holy Place, and, subsequent to his expulsion from Judah, the Temple had been rededicated. At the time, some of the Macabee patriots postulated that Antiochus was the desecrating power of Daniel's prophecy. But this man could not have been the correct personage of the antichrist because Christ identified the abomination of desolation as future to His time:

> When ye therefore shall see the abomination of desolation, spoken of by Daniel the prophet, stand in the holy place, (whoso readeth, let him understand) (Matthew 24:15).

Further, Daniel identifies the little horn power as becoming *exceeding great* (Daniel 8:9). Greece, under Alexander the Great, is described only as *very great* (Daniel 8:8). Hardly could Antiochus Epiphanes, who is scarcely remembered in history, be described as greater than Alexander the Great, whose name almost every school child recognizes. Nevertheless, many accepted this unscriptural proposition proposed by de Alcasar.

On the other hand, another young Jesuit, Francisco Ribera, postulated an interpretation which has become known as the futurist view of prophetic interpretation. This view claimed that a satanic individual would appear just before the end of the world. He would sit in the rebuilt temple in Jerusalem, blaspheming and desecrating it. Yet such an interpretation cannot stand in the light of biblical statements. John identified many antichrists in his day:

> Little children, it is the last time: and as ye have heard that antichrist shall come, even now are there many antichrists; whereby we know that it is the last time (1 John 2:18).

Luther, along with most of the Reformers, identified the antichrist not as one person but as the papal system which developed out of the apostasies of the early Christian church. This concept of prophetic interpretation was built upon the historicist view of prophetic understanding. It correctly identified the antichrist as developing even in John's day and continuing down through the Middle Ages to reach its climax of deception at the very end of time. It is not one man but a succession of men in the personage of the pope, as head of the papal system.

The futurist view was revived by the efforts of the leaders of Anglo-Catholicism in England in the early part of the nineteenth century. There was a determined effort by some to facilitate the reunification of the Church of England with the Church of Rome. Many earnest Anglicans rose up against such efforts, pointing out that the Church of Rome was the antichrist. One of the leaders of the Anglo-Catholic movement at Oxford University, Professor Morford, dusted off the thesis of Ribera and declared that the antichrist was yet to come, thus directing attention away from the papacy.

Many students of theology uncritically accepted this erroneous theology. Prominent among them was John Darby who was later to found the Plymouth Brethren Church. He in turn brought the concepts of futurism to America where they were accepted very readily by some conservative Protestants. When the well-known Texas lawyer, Charles Schofield, accepted Christianity, he imbibed the futuristic views. When he published his *Schofield Bible*, his extensive notes fully incorporated these futuristic interpretations. These Bibles were sold by the millions, especially in the southern part of the United States, but, indeed, all over America and in some other parts of the world. Today the influence of the *Schofield Bible* is vastly in excess of the influence of any seminary ever established in America.

By accepting the Jesuit concepts of futuristic interpretation, those who espouse the *new theology* fail to emphasize the identification of the antichrist as the papacy. Somewhat presumptuously they argue that such identification is a polemic that militates against Christian unity and the love of Christ. It is unfortunately true that there have been times when Seventh-day Adventists have used such polemics in their efforts to identify the Roman Catholic Church and the papacy as the antichrist. It is our belief that this is a very sensitive issue that needs to be presented with the understanding that many of God's people are still in the Roman Catholic faith.

> And I heard another voice from heaven, saying, Come out of her, *my people*, that ye be not partakers of her sins, and that ye receive not of her plagues (Revelation 18:4, emphasis added).

This sensitive love for God's sheep still in the Roman Catholic faith cannot, however, remove our responsibility to condemn the Satan-led system of the papacy and point out the eternal danger of adherence to its teachings and ceremonies.

Those who hold to this futuristic concept of the Bible also tend to deny the day-year principle of prophetic interpretation. At best they employ both the day-year historical interpretation of prophecy while at the same time accepting a literal interpretation of prophecy. They interpret the 1260 days as a period representing three and a half literal years at the end of time in which the antichrist will reign and set up his desolation in Jerusalem. Futurists commonly employ what is called the gap theory in their interpretation of the 70-weeks prophecy of Daniel, chapter 9. It is usual to accept the day-year principle as applying to this time period. Thus the 70 weeks (490 days) is rightly interpreted as 490 years. It is usually agreed that the first 69 weeks (483 prophetic days or literal years) reaches to the time of Christ's earthly ministry. However, futurists, ignoring all logic, place the last week (seven prophetic days or 7 literal years) down at the end of time by postulating a gap of around 2,000 years between the fulfillment of the 69 weeks and the fulfillment of the 70th week of the prophecy. Seventh-day Adventists, following consistant principles of prophetic interpretations, have always proclaimed that the 70th week is contiguous with the 69 weeks. This is the time of Christ's three and a half years of ministry after His baptism. His crucifixion was followed by three and a half further years of probation for the Jewish nation before the gospel was taken to the Gentiles following the stoning of Stephen, the deacon. This interpretation reinforces the heavenly sanctuary message that is enshrined in Daniel 8:14 and in the book of Hebrews.

It is important to recognize also that those proclaiming the *new theology* have often claimed to believe the historicist view of biblical interpretation, while also seeing validity in the preterist and/or the futurist views.[1]

But such a composite view should not be accepted. Never can truth and error reside together. The early Christian church for many years kept Sunday sacred while also keeping the Sabbath, but inevitably it was the error which prevailed. So, too, in placing together these erroneous prophetic interpretational views, the error will prevail and the truth will eventually be lost. This has already been seen amongst many. Certainly the historicist view will be minimized and eventually rejected by those who hold to a pluralistic view of prophetic interpretation. Dr. Ford is a classic example of this.

In His love, God has given to us great warnings against apostasy and the apostate system. He now calls to those who are in bondage to pagan infiltration. Christians must come into the purity of His faith that they might fully reflect His character and present His glorious invitation to the world. Invariably there is neither a biblical nor theological reason to reject the clear testimony of the principles of prophetic interpretation as entrusted to and taught by the Seventh-day Adventist Church.

Endnote

[1]The historicist view holds that the time prophecies of Scripture were fulfilled prior to or at the beginning of the time of the end. The preterist view suggests that these prophecies were fulfilled prior to the first advent of Christ. The futurist view asserts that the fulfillment of the time prophecies are yet future and will be fulfilled by the appearance of the antichrist just prior to the return of Jesus.

11

The Spirit of Prophecy and the New Theology

For a remarkable period of time there were strenuous efforts by those who were introducing the *new theology* into our midst to convince their hearers and readers that they were preaching messages consistent with the writings of the Spirit of Prophecy. By careful and selective choice of passages and wresting the writings of Sister White, they were able to convince some that they were rediscovering God's truth. But upon close examination, it was found that every single major principle espoused by the *new theology* was inconsistent with the writings of Sister White.

Because Sister White's writings perfectly reflect the great messages of the Scriptures, it has not been surprising to the perceptive church member that the proponents of the *new theology* eventually were forced to disavow her prophetic gift. This disavowal had begun very subtly. At first, *new theology* proponents indicated that Sister White had been of great blessing and impact upon their lives. They indicated that she had been *perfect for her purpose*. When asked to define what the purpose of her messages were, we were told that they were designed "to give counsel and guidance to the church."

It was frequently stated that she was not a theologian; that she may be wrong in facts of history and science; and that her messages are not doctrinal nor exegetical. Rather it was asserted that the writings of the Spirit of Prophecy are wonderful counsels. Thus these writings were effectively damned with faint praise. But even with such deceptive approaches, there was a limit to the length of time these men could conceal the reality of their rejection of Sister White's prophetic gift.

Now many supporters of the teachings of the *new theology* totally deny Sister White's role in the church, thus exposing their former sham. Some have gone to the extent of burning her writings or throwing them away. Others have given them away. One minister sold all his Spirit of Prophecy volumes declaring that he was merely upgrading his library! Some have even declared themselves to have a feeling of great freedom and relief from guilt now that they have ceased reading her counsels. This euphoria parallels the initial reaction of Adam and Eve after they had partaken of the forbidden fruit. But sadly, ultimately, the *new theology* has brought grief and alienation.

Open denial of the Spirit of Prophecy frequently commenced with the claim that the individual was no longer chained to the legalistic concepts that have proscribed the wearing of jewelry and of colorful cosmetics. Later those of this view professed to see nothing wrong with the taking of a little alcohol. Thus step by step they were drawn away from the beautiful principles of righteousness by which Christ frees us from the snares of Satan. Many of these individuals later found their marriages in shatters and have experienced the terrible trauma of separation and divorce. To this tragedy has been added the concomitant negative psychological impact upon the precious children whom God has entrusted to them. This rejection of divine counsel has turned into terrible bondage. Such have failed to discern the loving counsels of God through the Bible and the writings of Sister White.

These folk have also denied that the Seventh-day Adventist Church is the remnant church of God; therefore, they have rejected the most striking evidence of Scripture which testifies that God's final people will be blessed with the Spirit of Prophecy:

> And the dragon was wroth with the woman, and went to make war with the remnant of her seed, which keep the commandments of God, and have the testimony of Jesus Christ (Revelation 12:17).

> And I fell at his feet to worship him. And he said unto me, See thou do it not: I am thy fellowservant, and of thy brethren that have the testimony of Jesus: worship God: for the testimony of Jesus is the spirit of prophecy (Revelation 19:10).

In rejecting the Spirit of Prophecy, the supporters of the *new theology* have ultimately rejected the Bible. We hear similar comments concerning the Bible as have been made regarding the Spirit of Prophecy. It, too, "is perfect for its purpose." Its purpose is to reveal salvation, it is asserted, but it is in error in science and in history. Indeed many go to great lengths to disavow the fact that the time frame since Creation week is approximately 6,000 years. They frequently question the biblical facts revealed concerning Noah's flood; subsequently the meanings of many of the great events that are described in the Word of God have been altered. Even though these individuals see the Bible as inspired in its presentations of salvation principles, in the ultimate, even this fact is frequently rejected. For example, they deny the perfect state of God's remnant:

> The remnant of Israel shall not do iniquity, nor speak lies; neither shall a deceitful tongue be found in their mouth: for they shall feed and lie down, and none shall make them afraid (Zephaniah 3:13).

We recall a young man who, while a student in one of our colleges, taught the concept that the Bible is perfect in its revelation of salvation principles alone. He had decided to return to the Seventh-day Adventist college for an additional year prior to attending a secular university where he proposed to study for a medical degree. His motivation was the desire that such a preparation would give him the foundation in the Word of God that he needed to be a truly Christian physician. But in that year he lost his faith. He rightly argued that if the Bible was inaccurate in history and science then there was considerable doubt that its presentation of salvation principles was accurate. He reasoned logically that if the Bible was unreliable in that which he could investigate directly, it was likely to be similarly unreliable in its pronouncements upon that which he could not directly investigate. This young man had formed a logical conclusion. Tragically, his year at college, rather than strengthening his faith in God and His Word, led him away from them. We need not indicate what an anguish this course of events produced in the hearts of his godly parents. He left the Lord and, to the best of our knowledge, has never again returned to Him.

Questions have been raised concerning degrees and levels of Inspiration. These questions are not new. From time to time it has been said that Sister White possessed a lesser Inspiration than the Bible writers; such views tended to diminish the authority of the counsels of Sister White; indeed that was their designated purpose. This view was *supported* by statements made by Sister White herself. In these passages, she states that her writings are a lesser light to lead to the greater light of the Bible. She also counseled that the reader refrain from putting her writings above the Bible. Further, it has been rightly stated that her writings are not part of Scripture. From these facts, it has been inferred that they are thus less authoritative. Again Sister White referred to herself as a messenger rather than a prophetess, and some have used this description as evidence that her Inspiration is of a lower level. Carefully, these people have ignored those statements where Sister White stated that her roll was more than that of a prophetess. These statements have been so misinterpreted that many have been led to reject the messages of the Spirit of Prophecy.

A further effort to diminish the divine authority of Sister White's counsel has been made by suggesting that she was fully inspired when she received her messages in visions or dreams, but that at other times she merely expressed her own ideas. To apply this criterion to Sister White would require that same measuring rod to be applied to the Bible. If this criterion was accepted, then most of the Bible would be rejected. Indeed, frequently that has been the end of the road for those who have dared to challenge the heavenly authority of Sister White's messages.

But the remnant church must have as one of its identifying characteristics, the Spirit of Prophecy:

> And the dragon was wroth with the woman, and went to make war with the remnant of her seed, which keep the commandments of God, and *have the testimony of Jesus Christ* (Revelation 12:17, emphasis added).

> And I fell at his feet to worship him. And he said unto me, See thou do it not: I am thy fellowservant, and of thy brethren that *have the testimony of Jesus*: worship God: for *the testimony of Jesus is the spirit of prophecy* (Revelation 19:10, emphasis added).

The Lord has promised the prophetic gift in the last days:

> And it shall come to pass afterward, that I will pour out my spirit upon all flesh; and your sons and your daughters shall prophesy, your old men shall dream dreams, your young men shall see visions (Joel 2:28).

There are those who have suggested that much of Sister White's counsel may be disregarded with impunity, since she was a noncanonical prophet. Such a conclusion ignores the fact that Christ declared that no prophet was greater than John the Baptist. Yet he, too, was a noncanonical prophet, since he wrote no portion of Scripture.

It is our belief that in these last days God would not entrust His messages to a minor prophet. In the kingdom, it is our expectation that Sister White will be seen to have been a major prophet. We believe that degrees of Inspiration have no validity. Either she was a true prophet, fully inspired, or she was a false prophet, inspired only by Satan. The acceptance of the prophetic gift in the ministry of Sister White is essential not only to the preparation of God's people for the eternal kingdom but to the acceptance of the Scriptures as inspired.

12

Perfection and the New Theology

I n some circles in the Seventh-day Adventist Church, the word, *perfection,* has become a taboo word. The *new theology* has contributed much to this unfortunate situation. Those who accept the call of the Bible and Spirit of Prophecy to holy living are intimidated by fear of being labeled as legalists and perfectionists.

As we review the Bible, we notice that the word, *perfect,* is used freely. Many, seeking to divert attention from the biblical concept of character perfection, have claimed that the Bible means maturity when the term, *perfection,* is used. We are not questioning this possible meaning in certain passages. However, we would point out the inappropriateness of this meaning in some passages. Let us take the ultimate call of Christ:

> Be ye therefore perfect, even as your Father in heaven is perfect (Matthew 5:48).

If we want to transfer the word, *perfect,* to *maturity* in this text, we believe we would be in terrible difficulty. When Adam and Eve were created, they were perfect. But all their faculties were capable of development. They were perfect but immature. So it is when we first permit the fullness of the power of Christ in our lives. We may be perfect but, almost certainly, we are very immature. God's perfection is infinite. We can never achieve that, for it would require infinite knowledge. Not even the angels have such perfection. Certainly, in the kingdom of the redeemed, we will never achieve that level of maturity. But the Lord has promised His power to give us victory over sin. Ours is a *dependent* perfection, depending upon the power of Christ moment by moment for victory over temptation.

Too many within our church confound the words *perfection* and *perfectionism*. Of note is the fact that scores of times Sister White uses the term, *perfect*. She consistently upholds it as a God-given gift to every submitted Christian. Further, she states that God not only imputes perfection but He also imparts it. On one occasion only do we know of Sister White's use of the term, *perfectionism*. That statement is in *Early Writings*:

> God will not entrust the case of His precious flock to men whose mind and judgment have been weakened by former errors that they have cherished, such as so-called *perfectionism* and Spiritualism, and who, by their course while in these errors, have disgraced themselves and brought reproach upon the cause of truth (*Early Writings*, p. 101, emphasis added).

In more recent editions of *Early Writings* is recorded the divine understanding to which Sister White is referring:

> Some of the early Adventists, shortly after the 1844 experience, lost their hold on God and drifted into fanaticism. Ellen White met these extremists with a "thus saith the Lord." She rebuked those who taught a state of perfection in the flesh and therefore could not

sin. Of such Mrs. White later wrote: they held that those who are sanctified cannot sin. And this naturally led to the belief that the affections and desires of the sanctified ones were always right, and never in danger of leading them into sin. In harmony with these sophistries, they were practicing the worst sins under the garb of sanctification, and through their deceptive, mesmeric influence were gaining a strange power over some of their associates, who did not see the evil of these apparently beautiful but seductive theories. . . . Clearly the deceptions of these false teachers were laid open before me, and I saw the fearful account that stood against them in the book of records, and the terrible guilt that rested upon them for professing complete holiness while their daily acts were offensive in the sight of God (*Early Writings*, p. 301).

Thus this movement of the 1850s to which Sister White referred was very similar to the holy flesh movement of 1900, in which people were claiming perfection of the flesh while practicing the greatest abominations.

The center of the 1888 message in Minneapolis, and the righteousness by faith messages that were presented afterward, was an understanding of the gospel in the light of Calvary in which the cross was seen as central to both justification and Christian victory. These messages were designed to remove the legalism by which man's efforts were presented, albeit unwittingly, as dominant to his salvation. Rather, in the light of Calvary, it was evident that our justification and our sanctification (Ephesians 5:25-27; Hebrews 10:10; Hebrews 13:12) could be understood only in the context of what God has done for us through His Son, Jesus Christ.

In the Seventh-day Adventist Church, the issue of perfection and perfectionism has been confounded. Colin preached in Holland some time ago upon the topic, *Perfection or Perfectionism*. Prior to his presentation, he desired to ascertain that the material he was using from the Bible and the Spirit of Prophecy was accurately translated in the Dutch equivalents. After comparing all the texts, the translator assured him that the meanings were identical. But when they examined the statement concerning perfectionism in *Early Writings*, the translator expressed alarm, for he had discovered that the Dutch translators had translated the word *perfectionism* by use of the Dutch equivalent of *teaching perfection*. This translation seriously distorted the meaning which Sister White had intended. Therefore, it would be understandable that our Dutch brethren would have no concept of the real meaning of the warning that Sister White provided in this passage.

Perfectionism is built upon the merits of man's work. True Christian character perfection, on the other hand, is totally at odds with the legacy of perfectionism. It is a free gift of God, provided through the merits, sacrifice, and ministry of His Son. Perfection is available to all who will lovingly respond to the call of Christ upon their lives.

Perfectionism teaches that man may reach a point in this life beyond which no further growth in sanctification is possible, for we have reached obedience to the infinite will of God. It further claims that man cannot fall from this state. Both these claims are not founded upon Scripture and thus must be rejected.

In more recent years, theories related to the doctrine of perfection, which are more subtle than those of the *new theology*, have entered into the Seventh-day Adventist Church. It is now widely proclaimed that we sin because we are sinful. We are not sinful because we sin. This is a modification of the Augustinian concept of original sin. It fails to differentiate between the nature which we inherit and the character which we developed. We are born with a sinful nature, and through the power of Christ alone may we develop a perfect character. Unconverted, we follow the inclinations of our sinful nature and are impotent to resist the temptations of Satan. But when converted, the power of Christ provides victory, empowering the development of a perfect character.

Associated with the view that we sin because we are sinful has developed the notion that Christ had a composite human nature, one which displayed the characteristics of that possessed by Adam both before and after the Fall. An analysis of this fence-sitting position usually reveals that the proposer believes that Christ inherited the physical fallen nature of Adam but possessed an unfallen moral nature. This proposition, found neither in Scripture nor the Spirit of Prophecy, is most dangerous. Again we would emphasize that unthinkingly its supporters are accepting the dualistic theories of Greek paganism. Seventh-day Adventists have never separated the soul from the body. Our health reform message is based upon our rejection of dualism. It is totally impossible for one's physical nature to be fallen and his moral nature unfallen. Either man possesses a fallen nature or an unfallen nature. There can be no composite nature. Again it needs to be emphasized that character is distinct from nature. Christ possessed a fallen human nature[1] but His character was ever perfect. In this He provided an example to us.

> For even hereunto were ye called: because Christ also
> suffered for us, leaving us an example, that ye should
> follow his steps: Who did no sin, neither was guile
> found in his mouth (1 Peter 2:21, 22).

That Jesus possessed a fallen nature is seen by His collapse when bearing the cross. This was the response of a nature weakened by 4,000 years of sin.

It is important to delineate that which biblical perfection is not:

1. *Perfection is not holy flesh.* Our sinful, fallen nature will not be changed until this mortal puts on immortality and this corruptible puts on incorruption at the return of Jesus Christ. This change is termed, *glorification.* But through the power of Jesus, God's children will gain victory over every temptation of Satan, not through human power but through the power of the divine.

2. *Perfection in no wise ensures immunity from future sin.* Victory today is no guarantee of victory for tomorrow. Indeed, we are to become converted daily, so that we may possess the power of the indwelling Christ. It is possible to fall, as all of us can sadly testify. But how wonderful it is for us to know that if we sin we have an Advocate with the Father, Jesus Christ the righteous (1 John 2:1). Nevertheless, the same text of Scripture calls to God's children to cease from sin.

Some have asked us questions such as "Are you perfect?" or "Do you know anyone who is perfect?" These are questions that are not man's to answer and thus are most improper. Job was a perfect man:

> And the Lord said unto Satan, Hast thou considered my servant Job, that there is none like him in the earth, a perfect and an upright man, one that feareth God, and escheweth evil (Job 1:8)?

But Job dared not claim such perfection. Indeed, he was totally oblivious of it.

> If I justify myself, mine own mouth shall condemn me: if I say, I am perfect, it shall also prove me perverse. Though I were perfect, yet would I not know my soul: I would despise my life (Job 9:20, 21).

The saints will be the last to boast of their worthiness for heaven. They will ever sense their utter unworthiness.

God could never entrust the giving of the final invitation to the world to a people of flawed and defective character. Many listeners would turn away from the message, not because they disbelieved the message, but because of inconsistencies in the lives of the messengers. God's final invitation to the world could not be degraded before the inhabitants of the world by its presentation from the lips of those still living lives of sin. All inhabitants of the earth must receive an authentic invitation to make their decision for eternity.

Indeed, the return of Jesus is contingent upon the perfection of His people. As Seventh-day Adventists, we have often concentrated on the wrong issues. We have feverishly designed programs to encourage our people to witness to their faith; but, with the tragic Laodicean complacency amongst us, few are interested in sharing the wonderful salvation that God has provided for us. Rather our efforts need to be directed towards reformation. When this is accomplished in the hearts of God's people, they *will* present His truth to the world. No designed program will then be required to urge them to duty. The infilling of the Holy Spirit will be their supreme motivation.

In recent times, with the doctrinal and lifestyle dissonance within our church, there have been strong cries for unity. But few understand the only basis upon which the return of the Lord will take place. Jesus will not return until God's people have been sanctified by the truth. For this alone results in the unity that allows God to empower His people to give the loud cry of Revelation 18:1-5. This gospel reaches to every nook and cranny of the world, and, then, our Lord and Saviour will appear to redeem His waiting saints.

We know that Jesus will not come until the gospel commission has been taken to every nation, kindred, tongue, and people (Matthew 24:14). Though there have been remarkable efforts by the Seventh-day Adventist Church to share this message around the world, we still must acknowledge the reality that the overwhelming majority of the inhabitants of this world have never heard the name, *Seventh-day Adventist*, much less the thrilling truths that God has entrusted to us.

Yet we know that Christ's invitation will not be given to all the world until God's people are empowered by the Holy Spirit. We have been promised a power greater than Pentecost. So dramatic was the presentation of the message under the power of Pentecost that Paul was able to report before the fall of Jerusalem that the gospel, "was preached to every creature which is under heaven" (Colossians 1:23).

Yet we know that we will not receive the Holy Spirit until God's people are unified:

> And when the day of Pentecost was fully come, they were all with one accord in one place (Acts 2:1).

That same unity is necessary at the end time before God can entrust us with the Holy Spirit.

But how can we have that unity? We have listened to a number of sermons over the last few years promising unity. All have addressed the beautiful message of Jesus in His prayer,

> That they all may be one; as thou, Father, art in me, and I in thee, that they also may be one in us: that the world may believe that thou hast sent me (John 17:21).

All the sermons to which we have listened have failed to look at the sole basis upon which this unity will be achieved. So important is this principle that Christ refers to it twice in His prayer:

> Sanctify them through thy truth: thy Word is truth (John 17:17).

> And for their sakes I sanctify myself, that they also might be sanctified through the truth (John 17:19).

Until God's people are sanctified, there will not be unity. Every other call is a call for a counterfeit unity, for such calls are predicated upon that which will destroy unity. Frequently these calls are calls to compromise, consensus, or to the silencing of truth. God cannot bring genuine unity under these circumstances. So important is this matter that Sister White wrote,

> Unity is the sure result of Christian perfection (Sanctified Life, p. 85).

Unity is not a goal, as it is so often presented, it is a natural result of Christian perfection. Sadly, the widespread teaching of the sin-and-live philosophy has reaped havoc and dissention. Only a full response to churchwide calls for revival, repentance, and reformation will result in unity. The return of Jesus depends upon it. Of course, not all church members will respond to Christ's call. The final shaking brought about by persecution will remove all who continue in their worldliness and selfishness.

Our emphasis upon the return of Jesus must be focused first upon a thorough understanding of God's truth. Only those filled with the Holy Spirit can obtain that understanding. God calls each one of us to study God's Word individually and in groups; learning it, understanding it, and then asking the Holy Spirit to translate its truths into the very fabric of our lives so that we might be sanctified and perfected.

The present attack upon the doctrine of perfection of character which is so rampant within our midst is the greatest barrier to church unity today. No other matter is doing more to hinder the return of Jesus than this Satan-inspired error. With great earnestness, simplicity, and humility we are to take hold of the promises of God, permitting Him to do for us that which we cannot do for ourselves. It is useless praying that we give our hearts to the Lord, for we cannot do that. But we can ask Christ to take our lives and do for us that which we cannot do for ourselves. He has promised that:

> There hath no temptation taken you but such as is common to man: but God is faithful, who will not suffer you to be tempted above that ye are able; but will with the temptation also make a way to escape, that ye may be able to bear it (1 Corinthians 10:13).

> Now unto him that is able to keep you from falling, and to present you faultless before the presence of his glory with exceeding joy (Jude 24).

Wherefore he is able also to save them to the uttermost that come unto God by him (Hebrews 7:25).

If we confess our sins, he is faithful and just to forgive us our sins and to cleanse us from all unrighteousness (1 John 1:9).

Whereby are given unto us exceeding great and precious promises: that by these ye might be partakers of the divine nature, having escaped the corruption that is in the world through lust (2 Peter 1:4).

He that overcometh . . . I will not blot out his name out of the book of life (Revelation 3:5).

She should be arrayed in fine linen, clean and white: for fine linen is the righteousness of the saints (Revelation 19:8).

Blessed are they that do His commandments, that they may have right to the tree of life (Revelation 22:14).

And they overcame him by the blood of the Lamb, and by the word of their tesimony; and they loved not their lives unto the death (Revelation 12:11).

Here is the patience of the saints: here are they that keep the commandments of God, and the faith of Jesus (Revelation 14:12).

Christ also suffered for us, leaving us an example, that we should follow his steps: who did no sin, neither was guile found in his mouth (1 Peter 2:21, 22).

Who gave Himself for us, that he might redeem us from all iniquity, and purify unto himself a peculiar people, zealous of good works (Titus 2:14).

Denying ungodliness and worldly lusts, we should live soberly, righteously, and godly, in this present world (Titus 2:12).

> Thou shalt keep this commandment without spot, unrebukeable, until the appearing of our Lord Jesus Christ (1 Timothy 6:14).

> Till we all come in the unity of faith, and of the knowledge of the Son of God, unto a perfect man, unto the measure of the statue of the fulness of Christ: That we henceforth be no more children, tossed to and fro, and carried about with every wind of doctrine, by the slight of men, and cunning craftiness, whereby they lay in wait to deceive (Ephesians 4:13, 14).

What wonderful assurance these verses offer. Sister White shares the strength of these promises.

> You have confessed your sins, and in heart put them away. You have resolved to give yourself to God. Now go to Him, and ask that He will wash away your sins and give you a new heart. Then believe that He does this because He has promised (Steps to Christ, pp. 49, 50).

We have barely begun to look at the wonderful promises of Christian victory and perfection that Christ has provided for those who allow Him to work His work of salvation. This is not legalism, for it depends not upon the merit of man but upon the merit of our Lord and Saviour, Jesus Christ; upon His death and ministry on behalf of each one of us. Christ will have a people who will fully reflect His character. God will have a faithful army, largely of youth, who will be entrusted with taking this glorious message to every corner of this world. They are people who have permitted Christ to perfect His righteousness in their lives. They give an authentic spirit-filled invitation to the entire inhabitants of the earth. They will follow the Lamb wherever He goes.

Endnote

[1]Sister White uses the term, *fallen,* or its equivalent, *sinful,* in relation to Jesus' nature on at least 40 occasions. Never once does she describe Christ's nature as *unfallen or sinless.* In the book, *Desire of Ages*, p. 117, she emphatically states that this included His moral worth.

This page intentionally left blank.

13

The Gospel and the New Theology

One of the doctrinal pillars of the *new theology* is the claim that the saints will continue to sin until Jesus comes. An intricate theological construct has been devised in order to support the error that it is impossible for humans to gain victory over sin in this life. This attack on Christian perfection is not new. In the eighteenth century, John Wesley had to meet it. One of the greatest opponents of the doctrine of Christian perfection at that time was the well-known theologian, Count von Zinzendorf. In commenting upon von Zinzendorf's views, Wesley had this to say:

> There is scarcely an expression in Holy Writ which has given more offence than this. The word perfect is what many cannot bear. The very sound of it is an abomination to them, and whosoever preacheth perfection . . . that it is obtainable in this life, runs great hazard of being counted by them, worse than a heathen man or a publican (John Wesley, *The Works of Wesley*, vol. 6., p. 1).

Still speaking of Count von Zinzendorf, Wesley continued:

> "No," says a great man. "This is an error of errors. I hate it from my heart. I pursue through all the world

with fire and sword this idea that you can overcome sin" (*ibid.*).

In response Wesley said,

"I say, why so vehement? Why are those who oppose salvation from sin, few excepted, so eager? In God's name, why are you so fond of sin? What has it ever done for you? What good is it ever likely to do for you in this world, or in the world to come? And why are you so violent against those who hope for a deliverance from it (*ibid.*)?

It is this concept, as enunciated by von Zinzendorf, that has severely damaged the concept of the gospel in the minds of many Seventh-day Adventists, for it also has been propounded by the proponents of the *new theology*. Earlier we detailed the understanding of the gospel enshrined in Lutheran theology and, alternatively, as espoused by the Roman Catholic bishops at the Council of Trent. It will be remembered that eventually the Council of Trent declared that the gospel included both justification and sanctification. This declaration has been used as ammunition to claim that the true gospel involving justification and sanctification is Catholic and Romanish. This charge is totally unfounded. The *sanctification* espoused by the Catholic Church is mediated by works (sacramentalism) whereas the Bible teaches sanctification by faith.

Some of the errors of the *new theology* attack the following truths concerning the gospel:

1. *Justification by faith is more than a forensic act of God.* The *new theology* proposes the notion that justification is an act of God, apart and separate from man. It is claimed that there is no subjective element in justification. Conversely, the Seventh-day Adventist message teaches that justification re-

quires entire surrender of the will. Without this surrender through the power of Christ, we cannot be justified. Improper applications of some of Paul's statements have been made. These include:

> But to him that worketh not, but believeth on him that justifieth the ungodly, his faith is counted for righteousness (Romans 4:5).

Using this text, some have claimed that Christ justifies ungodly men in their sins. It is denied that there is a change from sin unto righteousness in the converted individual. It has even been claimed that the only difference between the drunk in the gutter and the saved man is that the latter has accepted the justifying grace of Jesus.

Some go so far as to declare that all we have to do is to claim an intellectual belief in Christ. It is true that God justifies the ungodly, since all men are sinners. But He most decidedly will not justify a man who remains in that condition. Missionaries convert the heathen, but they are not converted while they continue their heathen practices. Jude specifically states that the ungodly will certainly not inherit the kingdom of God:

> To execute judgment upon all, and to convince all that are ungodly among them of all their ungodly deeds which they have ungodly committed, and of all their hard speeches which ungodly sinners have spoken against him (Jude 15).

Jesus, Himself, clarified the issue:

> I came not to call the righteous, but sinners *to repentance* (Luke 5:32, emphasis added).

Justification requires transformation of the life.

> For not the hearers of the law are just before God, but the doers of the law shall be justified (Romans 2:13).

> Let the wicked forsake his way, and the unrighteous man his thoughts: and let him return unto the Lord, and he will have mercy upon him; and to our God, for he will abundantly pardon (Isaiah 55:7).

> Keep thee far from a false matter; and the innocent and righteous slay thou not: for I will not justify the wicked (Exodus 23:7).

> He that covereth his sins shall not prosper: but whoso confesseth and forsaketh them shall have mercy (Proverbs 28:13).

Solomon condemned those who justify the wicked:

> He that justifieth the wicked, and he that condemneth the just, even they both are abomination to the Lord (Proverbs 17:15).

God cannot justify the sinner who does not forsake his sin. The grand principle of the new birth establishes the principle that God restores those whom He justifies that they might walk through the power of His grace.

Seventh-day Adventists believe that justification is empowered by God through His Son, Jesus Christ:

> Therefore being justified by faith, we have peace with God through our Lord Jesus Christ (Romans 5:1).

> Much more then, being now justified by his blood, we shall be saved from wrath through him (Romans 5:9).

> For in Jesus Christ neither circumcision availeth any thing, nor uncircumcision; but faith which worketh by love (Galatians 5:6).

> For by grace are ye saved through faith; and that not of yourselves: it is the gift of God (Ephesians 2:8).

God does not leave man wallowing in guilt, self-recrimination and low self-worth. He restores man to His image. This was central to the preaching of Dr. Elliot Waggoner and Elder

Alonzo Jones in their dynamic presentation of justification by faith.

2. *Sanctification is God's perfect work for man through the sacrifice and ministry of His Son, Jesus Christ.* There is no question that the greatest problem in the understanding of the adherents of the *new theology* is the result of the acceptance of the error that sanctification is man's imperfect work for God.

Colin once listened to a sermon where the preacher declared that to unite justification and sanctification together in the gospel was to commit spiritual adultery. Colin required great restraint in not challenging such a blasphemous statement during the service itself. Perhaps he should have. At the conclusion of the service, however, he explained to the preacher that there was a grave problem because of his erroneous view of sanctification. Colin agreed with the preacher that justification is God's perfect work for man through His Son, Jesus Christ. He disagreed, however, with the preacher's implied concept of sanctification. The preacher believed sanctification to be man's imperfect work for God. When Colin assured him that the Bible taught that sanctification, like justification, was God's perfect work for man through His Son, Jesus Christ, the preacher retorted, "Theologians no longer see it that way." Colin responded, "It is time to ignore the surmising of men and to return to Bible definitions." Incredibly the speaker's catchcry had been "The Bible only!" Yet he had discarded the Bible truth for the errors of mere man. The preacher's startling statement would only have been accurate if his erroneous belief concerning sanctification were correct.

Sanctification is bestowed by faith alone, not by works. Works, however, are the inevitable evidence of a holy life. There is no faith without good works. Bible believing Seventh-day Adventists accept that which faithful Christians down through the ages have always believed, that sanctification is God's gift of holiness to those who surrender their lives to Him. The Lord, Himself, declared to Paul that sanctification, like justification, is by faith in Him:

> To open their eyes, and to turn them from darkness to light, and from the power of Satan unto God, that they may receive forgiveness of sins, and inheritance among them which are *sanctified by faith* that is in me (Acts 26:18, emphasis added).

Further, the same sacrifice of Christ that justifies, also sanctifies:

> By the which will we are sanctified through the offering of the body of Jesus Christ once for all (Hebrews 10:10).

> Wherefore Jesus also, that he might sanctify the people with his own blood, suffered without the gate (Hebrews 13:12).

> Husbands, love your wives, even as Christ also loved the church, and gave himself for it; that he might sanctify and cleanse it with the washing of water by the word, that he might present it to himself a glorious church, not having spot, or wrinkle, or any such thing; but that it should be holy and without blemish (Ephesians 5:25-27).

The Bible is so rich in assurances of the sanctifying power of God that it is difficult to understand how this matter could be denied or misunderstood. Let us note the following references:

> Now Joshua was clothed with filthy garments, and stood before the angel. And he answered and spake

unto those that stood before him, saying, Take away the
filthy garments from him. And unto him he said, Behold, I have caused thine iniquity to pass from thee, and
I will clothe thee with change of raiment (Zechariah 3:3,
4).

Teaching us that, denying ungodliness and worldly
lusts, we should live soberly, righteously, and godly, in
this present world; looking for that blessed hope, and
the glorious appearing of the great God and our Saviour
Jesus Christ; who gave himself for us, that he might
redeem us from all iniquity, and purify unto himself a
peculiar people, zealous of good works (Titus 2:12-14).

For it is God which worketh in you both to will and
to do of his good pleasure (Philippians 2:13).

How much more shall the blood of Christ, who
through the eternal Spirit offered himself without spot
to God, purge your conscience from dead works to
serve the living God? (Hebrews 9:14).

Let us draw near with a true heart in full assurance
of faith, having our hearts sprinkled from an evil conscience, and our bodies washed with pure water
(Hebrews 10:22).

Whereby are given unto us exceeding great and precious promises: that by these ye might be partakers of
the divine nature, having escaped the corruption that is
in the world through lust (2 Peter 1:4).

Blessed is the man that endureth temptation: for
when he is tried, he shall receive the crown of life, which
the Lord hath promised to them that love him (James
1:12).

This I say then, Walk in the Spirit, and ye shall not
fulfil the lust of the flesh (Galatians 5:16).

Here is the patience of the saints: here are they that
keep the commandments of God, and the faith of Jesus
(Revelation 14:12).

But we are bound to give thanks alway to God for
you, brethren beloved of the Lord, because God hath

from the beginning chosen you to salvation through sanctification of the Spirit and belief of the truth (2 Thessalonians 2:13).

How rich are God's promises of sanctification. Sanctification is all of Him. There is nothing that we can do of ourselves but ask Him to take our lives and work His work of grace in them.

I am the vine, ye are the branches: He that abideth in me, and I in him, the same bringeth forth much fruit: for without me ye can do nothing (John 15:5).

It is certainly the power of Jesus working through man that restores man from sin unto sanctification.

Make you perfect in every good work to do his will, working in you that which is well pleasing in his sight, through Jesus Christ; to whom be glory for ever and ever (Hebrews 13:21).

This is the glorious message of sanctification. In the power of the gospel, man is restored by God, ready to live with holy angels and the unfallen beings of the universe.

3. *The gospel is justification and sanctification.* It is true that the concept of justification by faith alone was the dominant theology of most leaders of the sixteenth-century Reformation. But the concept of justification *alone* is not enshrined in the Bible. The word, *alone,* has been added by human assumption.

Seventh-day Adventists owe a great debt of gratitude to John Wesley who extended the Reformational principles of the gospel to include God's power to sanctify His people in addition to His power to justify. This is built upon the faith of Jesus. In contrast, the Roman Catholic concept of sanctification is built upon creedalism and human works.

Indeed, Scripture frequently links justification with sanctification in the gospel. Here are just some of these statements:

> To open their eyes, and to turn them from darkness to light, and from the power of Satan unto God, that they may receive forgiveness of sins [justification], and inheritance among them which are sanctified by faith that is in me (Acts 26:18).

> If we confess our sins, he is faithful and just to forgive us our sins [justification], and to cleanse us from all unrighteousness [sanctification] (1 John 1:9).

> There is therefore now no condemnation to them which are in Christ Jesus [justification], who *walk* not after the flesh, but after the Spirit [sanctification]. For the law of the Spirit of life in Christ Jesus hath made me free from the law of sin and death. For what the law could not do, in that it was weak through the flesh, God sending his own Son in the likeness of sinful flesh, and for sin, condemned sin in the flesh [justification]: that the righteousness of the law might be fulfilled in us, who walk not after the flesh, but after the Spirit [sanctification] (Romans 8:1-4).

> He that is unjust, let him be unjust still: and he which is filthy, let him be filthy still: and he that is righteous [justified], let him be righteous [justified] still: and he that is holy [sanctified], let him be holy [sanctified] still (Revelation 22:11).

> Jesus answered, Verily, verily, I say unto thee, Except a man be born of water [justification] and of the Spirit [sanctification], he cannot enter into the kingdom of God (John 3:5).

Even in the Lord's prayer we find the "marriage" of justification and sanctification:

> And forgive us our debts [justification], as we forgive our debtors. And lead us not into temptation, but deliver us from evil [sanctification]: For thine is the

kingdom, and the power, and the glory, for ever. Amen
(Matthew 6:12, 13).

When the principles of sanctification are fully understood
as embracing the gift of God, then we recognize that the
gospel is all Christ's work in us. There is no merit or basis in
man's works for his salvation. But everyone who is justified
and sanctified by the sacrifice and ministry of Christ will
manifest good works. Then others will see these "good
works, and glorify your Father which is in heaven" (Matthew 5:16).

How accurately the gospel is presented by Sister White:

> If you give yourself to Him, and accept Him as your
> Saviour, then, sinful as your life may have been, for
> His sake you are accounted righteous. Christ's char-
> acter stands in place of your character, and you are
> accepted before God just as if you had not sinned.
> More than this, Christ changes the heart. He abides in
> your heart by faith (*Steps to Christ*, p. 62).

In inspired language, the justifying and sanctifying
grace of God is revealed. How rich, how full, how satisfy-
ing is the gospel of Jesus Christ! It is not built upon human
pride nor achievement, but there will be many battles to be
fought and won. There will be stiff warfare against Satan.
There will be strong effort, but the power of victory is
entirely generated by God through Christ. It was not an
impotent gospel of which Paul wrote.

> For I am not ashamed of the gospel of Christ: for it
> is the power of God unto salvation to every one that
> believeth; to the Jew first, and also to the Greek
> (Romans 1:16).

The God we serve is all-powerful, He is all-suffi-
cient. He not only has the power to redeem us from

the condemnation of sin, He provides the power to preserve us from sin and its guilt.

This page intentionally left blank.

14

Reaping a Harvest

How does one expose the *new theology* for what it really is? There is no easy way, for it is a masterpiece of Satan. It is so beautifully masked in loving concern. It is not surprising then that even faithful leadership has been "powerless to stop the rushing torrent of iniquity" (*Testimonies for the Church,* vol. 5, p. 210).

Sadly, some in leadership responsibilities have supported and encouraged the deadly infiltration of the *new theology* into the hearts and lives of God's people. Such leaders have often put loyal pastors, other leaders, and laity on the defensive by accusing them of criticism, bitterness, and un-Christlikeness. Thus faithful servants have frequently felt that they must lower the voice of their concerns to a whisper to show their loyalty to their colleagues and to the church. Even for laity, it has not been easy to raise the alarm. Some have done so at the expense of their leadership roles and influence in the local church. Some have done so in the face of threat to their church membership.

In places like Australia and New Zealand, those faithful to God's truth have been discredited by the term, CB's (concerned brethren). Hardly can an individual and his influence be more quickly discredited than by this classification. It is not uncommon to hear it said that the CB's have done far more damage to the church than the adherents of the *new theology*. It is not hard to imagine that it takes more than ordinary courage to stand openly against the *new theology*, when any level of protest quickly tarnishes the reputation of the individual. Yet the command of the Lord is,

> No longer consent to listen without protest to the perversion of truth (*Selected Messages*, vol. 1, p. 196).

It is inevitable that the protesting of the *new theology*, however lovingly and caringly it is done, will be seen as bringing division. This in turn leads the faithful ones to be seen as disruptive elements in the church. Frequently such are told that it is not their beliefs, but it is the way they do it. Faithful people must not be intimidated by such false accusations. There is no "right way." God warns,

> If God abhors one sin above another, of which His people are guilty, it is doing nothing in case of an emergency. Indifference and neutrality in a religious crisis is regarded of God as a grievous crime and equal to the very worst type of hostility against God (*Testimonies for the Church*, vol. 3, p. 281).

But to honor God will inevitably lead to opposition. Human nature has not changed from the days of Christ.

> The Prince of Peace, He was yet the cause of division. He who came to proclaim glad tidings and to create hope and joy in the hearts of the children of men, opened a controversy that burns deep and arouses intense passion in the human heart. (*Acts of the Apostles*, p. 84).

The followers of Christ will not find it different, and the most intense opposition will come from unfaithful members in the church. Jesus, however, gives us assurance.

> Verily, verily, I say unto you, Whatsoever ye shall ask the Father in my name, he will give it you (John 16:23).

The defection of unfaithful church members as a result of truth being preached with clarity will be threatening, but God has promised,

> But there are men who will receive the truth, and these will take the places made vacant by those who become offended and leave the truth. . . . Men of true Christian principle will take their place, and will become faithful, trustworthy householders, to advocate the word of God in its true bearings, and in its simplicity. The Lord will work so that the disaffected ones will be separated from the true and loyal ones. . . . The ranks will not be diminished. Those who are firm and true will close up the vacancies that are made by those who become offended and apostatize (*Maranatha*, p. 200).

In the face of apostasy, it is sin and cowardice to remain silent. The blood of innocent souls, victims of the sin-and-live theology, will be upon the shoulders of those who fail to give the warning.

> Here we see that the church—the Lord's sanctuary—was the first to feel the stroke of the wrath of God. The ancient men, those to whom God had given great light and who had stood as guardians of the spiritual interests of the people had betrayed their trust. They had taken the position that we need not look for miracles and the marked manifestation of God's power as in former days. Times have changed. These words strengthen their unbelief, and they say: The Lord will not do good, neither will He do evil. He is too merciful

to visit His people in judgment. Thus "Peace and safety" is the cry from men who will never again lift up their voice like a trumpet to show God's people their transgressions and the house of Jacob their sins. These dumb dogs that would not bark are the ones who feel the just vengeance of an offended God (*Testimonies for the Church*, vol. 5, p. 211).

What makes it so difficult for leaders to deal with the *new theology*? Our experience indicates a number of factors.

1. Some leaders, themselves, are less than clear on the foundational truths of the remnant church. They may perceive vaguely that something is not right, but the enormity of the eternal loss is not remotely realized. Thus when concerns come to the conference, *new theology* teaching pastors are often told simply to be careful, often with the assurance that leadership is fully behind them.

2. Most administrators are imprisoned by the number of committees that they must attend. Thus their own searching for truth is spasmodic.

3. The official Seventh-day Adventist statement of beliefs is couched in such a way that pivotal doctrines such as victorious Christian living, the nature of Christ, and the Atonement are left sufficiently general that all but the most rabid *new theology* teachers can give confident assent to them. Thus it is hard to take strong action against them.

4. Many *new theology* ministers preach neutral themes. They avoid present truth yet do not directly teach error. As the servant of the Lord has said, this opens the door to Satan.

There are many precious truths contained in the Word of God, but it is "present truth" that the flock needs now. I have seen the danger of the messengers running off from the important points of present truth, to dwell upon subjects that are not calculated to unite the flock and sanctify the soul. Satan will here take every possible advantage to injure the cause.

But such subjects as the sanctuary in connection with the 2300 days, the commandments of God and the faith of Jesus, are perfectly calculated to explain the past Advent movement and show what our present position is, establish the faith of the doubting, and give certainty to the glorious future (*Early Writings,* p. 63).

5. The subtle sin-and-live theology has such appeal that it is not uncommon for the errant pastor to obtain major support from his congregation. He is easily able to fill his church board with eager supporters. Others are left out because they are thought to be legalists.

6. *New theology* teachers and preachers rarely have deep convictions; and, therefore, they avoid taking doctrinaire positions which can easily offend. They often appear to be very kind and long-suffering to those who oppose their errors. The faithful are made to appear to be the troublers of Israel. Like faithful Elijah of old, we need to proclaim,

I have not troubled Israel; but thou, and thy father's house, in that ye have forsaken the commandments of the Lord, and thou hast followed Baalim (1 Kings 18:18).

7. The message of *new theology* pastors is often seen as Christ-centered and loving. Yet the very life, teachings, and ministry of Christ is despised by these people.

It is usually because of these situations that pastors and teachers who dare to lead their flocks in their false views are rarely disciplined until the fruitage of their preaching is fully developed. By this time major, maybe irreversible, damage has been done. It is rather like the unobservant home owner who does not know there are termites in his home until the house suddenly collapses.

There is no way one can preach the sin-and-live theology without eventually falling into deep sin. Thus many of those, enamored with the *new theology*, evidence the emptiness of their *love* theology by their infidelity to their wives, marital breakup, and even drunkenness. The carnage in this area is horrendous. At the point of revelation of these grossly sinful courses, action is taken. Even then, it has been our experience that many of the members are so mesmerized that the conference is accused of being unloving and unforgiving. Too often, however, leaders taking such action do not recognize the deeper theological issues that have led, like an irresistible force, to the committing of gross sin.

The reader may well ask what are the telltale signs of a teacher or pastor who has leanings toward the *new theology*. These pointers do not suggest that the teacher or pastor is necessarily aware of his allegiance to the *new theology*. Many would deny it strenuously.

1. If, after listening to three or so sermons, you do not know what the pastor believes or where he stands, it is likely that he does not have true convictions concerning truth.

2. If the theme of the sermons is constantly love outside the context of God's law, certainly he is strongly drawn to the *new theology*.

3. If the pastor emphasizes justification, the cross of Calvary, the mercy of God but ignores or minimizes sanctification, the high priestly ministry of Christ, and the justice of God: beware!

4. If the pastor shares no burden to call for revival, repentance, and reformation your church is in trouble.

5. If you do not hear messages on the great pillars of the Advent faith, and truth and doctrine is ignored, your pastor is not faithful to his charge.

6. If you could hear the same set of sermons in the Baptist Church, there is little doubt of the pastor's disloyalty to the Advent faith.

7. If the pastor is strongly interested in ecumenical issues, exchange of pulpits with those not of our faith, the ministerial fraternal in the town, but does little to initiate and inspire to outreach, witnessing, and evangelizing there is a serious problem.

8. If the pastor ignores, belittles, or rationalizes the Spirit of Prophecy, you can be assured he has no right to be a minister of God's church.

If we cannot or will not preach the clear truths of the Scriptures, we are unfit to be teachers or pastors of God's end-time church. Indeed, we are not worthy to be members of God's church.

Today we face the reality that almost half of our worldwide members and 60 percent of our members in North America are not at church on a given Sabbath. We face the reality that over 70 percent of our youth in North America are leaving the church. We know not what percentage of the rest are truly converted. Tithes and offerings do not keep up with membership increase and inflation. Too frequently our answer is lowered standards, greater worldly entertainment, ignoring of church discipline, and eclective beliefs. There are few sacrifices to be a church member.

The only answer to the eternally destructive *new theology* is to uphold the authentic Christ—the Christ of love, the Christ of truth, the Christ of purity, the Christ of whom the law is the transcript of His character, the all-powerful Christ. Satan and his agents must be unmasked for what they are, wolves in sheep clothing. We must expose Satan's master-piece of deception and see the *love* as unconcern, the *care* as indulgence, the *forgiveness* as condoning of sin, the *kindness* as self-exaltation, and the *nonjudgmental* approaches as weakness. True love cares enough to be concerned for the precious souls for whom Christ died.

Now is the time to cry aloud and spare not; to call sin by its right name; to be true to principle as the needle is to the pole; to stand though the heavens fall: to yield not to flattery, bribery, nor threatening; to lift up the banner of Prince Emmanuel; to be keepers of the faith; to die rather than knowingly commit one sin; to be watchmen on the walls of Zion. This is the time to call God's people to truth and righteousness through the blood of the Lamb. This is the time to prepare the way of the Lord, to make straight His pathway. Surely this is the time to hasten the return of Jesus and to proclaim the love, mercy, long-suffering, purity, justice, and soon coming of our blessed Lord and Saviour.

Some are afraid that many will withdraw from church fellowship if they preach the clear messages of the Seventh-day Adventist Church. But, to the contrary, the great loss of effective, practicing membership in the church is the result of presentations that do nothing to attract the vision of the members nor galvanize their energies to the mighty challenge of preparing the way of the Lord. Only a distinctive message will hold and attract men and women to the kingdom of heaven and to the Seventh-day Adventist Church.

We are encouraged by the increasing number of both denominational workers and laity who are ready to stand; to break free from their timidity and indifference. While apostasy will increase until the close of probation; nevertheless, the place of the unfaithful will be taken by new converts to the truth of Christ. Though our loyalty be severely tested, we do have the wonderful promise,

> And ye shall be hated of all men for my name's sake: but he that shall endure unto the end, the same shall be saved (Mark 13:13).

This page intentionally left blank.

Summary of Differences Between Biblical Truths and New Theology

Biblical Truths

New Theology

Nature of Man

1. Man born with evil tendencies. Isaiah 64:6; Romans 3:10; 3:23; 5:12; Genesis 6:23; Psalm 51:5; Ephesians 2:1-3; Romans 8:5-7.

1. Man was born with original sin.

2. Man chooses his eternal destiny. Romans 7:24; Joshua 24:15; Matthew 23:37; Ezekiel 18:20, 21; Revelation 22:17; Ezekiel 18:4.

2. Man's eternity is predestinated.

3. Conditional salvation. Deuteronomy 7:9; Joshua 22:5; James 1:12; 2:5; 1 Corinthians 2:9; Isaiah 64:4; 2 Timothy 4:8; John 3:16; Acts 16:31; 1 John 5:1-5; Psalm 103:11, 13, 17, 18; 1 John 1:7; John 14:15; Matthew 19:16, 17; Ezekiel 18:24; Galatians 2:17, 18; Exodus 20:6.

3. Once-saved-always-saved.

4. Saints can and will have victory over sin now. 1 Peter 1:22, 23; Titus 2:14; 1 Corinthians 10:13; John 5:14; 1 Corinthians 15:43; 1 John 2:1; Philippians 4:13; 1 John 5:2, 3; 1 John 3:9; Jeremiah 31:31-33; Jeremiah 1:12; Romans 8:9, Romans 12:2; Galatians 5:16; Ephesians 2:4-6; 5:27; Hebrews 8:10; 10:16; Jude 24.

4. Saints continue to sin until Jesus comes.

5. Denies perfectionism but not perfection. Job 1:1, 8; 1 John 2:29; 2 Corinthians 7:1; 2 Timothy 4:18; 2 Corinthians 2:14; 1 John 3:9; 1 John 5:18.

5. Denies both perfectionism and perfection.

6. New birth at conversion. Acts 9:4, 5, 22; Mark 1:8, 11; Matthew 3:11; John 3:1-7; 1 John 2:20; 1 John 5:18; 2 Corinthians 3:18; Romans 6:6, 7; Ezekiel 36:26, 27; Ephesians 4:22-24; Romans 12:2; Philippians 2:5; Psalm 40:8.

6. New birth sometime after conversion.

7. We are in Christ and Christ is in us. 1 John 2:5, 6; 3:24; 4:13, 15; Psalm 119:2, 3; 2 Corinthians 13:5; John 15:4-7; John 14:10.

7. We are in Christ but Christ is not in us.

Biblical Truths

New Theology

Nature of sin

1. Sin is volitional disobedience. Exodus 20:7; Leviticus 6:4; James 2:10; 4:17; John 9:41; 5:22; Acts 17:30; 1 Corinthians 15:34; Romans 6:16.

1. Sin results from human limitations.

2. All sin may and must be put away now. Galatians 5:16-24; 1 Peter 4:1; 2 Peter 2:14, 15; James 1:21; Romans 6:6, 7; Revelation 3:21; Romans 8:14; 1 Corinthians 15:34; Philippians 4:13; 1 Corinthians 15:57; Hebrews 7:25; Job 1:22; 1 John 3:8, 9; 3:6; 5:18; 1 John 3:3-7; Jude 24; Psalm 51:12; 2 Peter 3:9; Romans 8:7; Romans 8:5, 6.

2. Sin removed at the Second Coming.

3. One sin separates from Christ. Genesis 3:22-24; Numbers 20:11, 12.

3. We are not separated from God if the tenor of our life is right.

Nature of Christ

1. Christ was born sanctified but in sinful flesh.
Romans 1:3; 8:3; Hebrews 2:4-18; Luke 1:35; 1 Peter 4:1; Hebrews 4:15; John 1:1-3, 14; Galatians 4:4, 5; John 5:30.

1. Chirst was born in sinless flesh.

2. Christ is our Substitute and Example. 1 John 3:3; Hebrews 4:15, 16; 1 Peter 2:21-23; Isaiah 53:4, 5; 1 Corinthians 15:3, 22; Matthew 26:28; Hebrews 9:28; 1 John 3:5-7; Acts 20:28; 1 Peter 1:18, 19; 1 John 1:7; Romans 5:6; Acts 3:26; 2 Corinthians 4:10.

2. Christ is our Substitute but not our Example.

Sanctuary Truth

1. Atonement completed in the sanctuary. Leviticus 16:33.

1. Atonement completed on the cross.

2. Christ began His MHP ministry in 1844. Daniel 8:14.

2. Christ began His MHP ministry in A.D. 31.

3. Judgement of the living before the close of probation. Daniel 12:1; 7:22; 7:11; 7:26; Revelation 14:7.

3. Judgment of the living at the Second Coming.

Nature of Salvation

1. Justification requires the entire surrender of the will. Romans 2:13; Isaiah 55:7; Proverbs 28:13; Ephesians 2:8; Romans 5:1, 9.

1. Justification is a forensic act of God only.

Biblical Truths

New Theology

2. Sanctification is God's gift of holiness to man. Zechariah 3:3, 4; Titus 2:14; Philippians 2:13; Hebrews 9:14; 10:22; 2 Peter 1:10, 11; James 1:12; 1 John 5:4; Galatians 5:16; Revelation 14:12; Acts 15:9; James 1:3, 4; 1 Thessalonians 5:22, 23; John 15:5; Hebrews 13:21; Philippians 2:13; Revelation 22:11.

2. Sancification is man's imperfect works for God.

3. Gospel—Justification and Sanctification. Philippians 1:6; Romans 3:24; 1 Corinthians 1:30; 1 John 4:13; Acts 3:26; Romans 1:16; Titus 2:14; Philippians 2:13; Romans 5:9; Ephesians 5:25-27; Hebrews 10:10; 13:21; 9:14; Acts 26:18; Revelation 22:11; 1 Thessalonians 5:23; Zechariah 3:3, 4; 1 John 1:9; Romans 8:1-4; Matthew 7:21; Hebrews 5:9; 2 Thessalonians 2:13.

3. Gospel—Justification alone.

Old Testament Scriptural Index

New Testament Scriptural Index

This page intentionally left blank.

Spirit of Prophecy Index

Books by the Same Authors

Adventism Challenged, Book A . . . . .US$5.95

Adventism Challenged, Book B . . . . .US$5.95
Origins of current issues facing the Seventh-day Adventist Church.

Adventism Imperiled . . . . .US$5.95
Reveals the biblical principles of true Christian education.

Adventism Jeopardized . . . . .US$5.95
The bibical principles of mental health and family life.

Adventism Proclaimed . . . . .US$5.95
A Contemporary understanding of the four angels' messages of
Revelation, chapter 14:6-12 and 18:1-5.

Adventism Unveiled . . . . .US$5.95
The biblical foundation of the sanctuary message.

Adventism Vindicated . . . . .US$5.95
Answering the challenge to the biblical message of righteousness by
faith.

Keepers of the Faith . . . . .US$6.95
Proposed solutions to the ministerial dilemma in the Seventh-day
Adventist Church.

Youth, Do You Dare! . . . . .US$4.95
Gives insights to young people in helping them strenghen the dimen-
tions of the spiritual values in their lives.

Deceptions of the New Theology . . . . .US$6.95
Exposes the step-by-step process of the new theology as it gains
momentum in the final conflict. Excellent guidelines for identifying the
earmarks of the new theology.

I Would Like to Tell You More About . . .

College

An opportunity to learn in a country setting with Christ-centered classes, work education, and outreach ministries. Majors: Pastoral Evangelism, Christian Elementary and Secondary Education, Christian Business Administration, Bible Worker, Restaurant Management, Health Ministries, and Agricultural Ministries. Contact dean of college, **703-672-3100.**

Lifestyle Reconditioning Center

A friendly and relaxing atmosphere, with qualified health-care professionals skilled in promoting lifestyle intervention for those who suffer from heart disease, arthritis, cancer, diabetes, overweight, and other conditions. Phone **800-322-WELL.** City clinics are also sponsored and staffed. Capitol Health Center, 4807 42nd Place, Hyattsville, MD 20781, telephone **301-699-0700.** Jefferson Park Clinic, 2433 Jefferson Park Avenue, Charlottesville, VA 22903, telephone **804-295-2927.**

Bible Conferences

Meetings scheduled in various locations. Evangelism, doctrines, health seminars. Contact Hartland Bible Conference coordinator, **703-672-3100.**

Hartland Journal

Information about what God is doing for us, as well as articles on physical and spiritual health. Free to all interested.

Institute Publications

Books and inspirational cassettes and videos for serious Christians. Price list available. Visa and MasterCard accepted. Telephone **703-672-3566.**

Volunteer Opportunities

Short and long term opportunities available for those who would like to volunteer their time and talents in exchange for food, lodging, and blessings from fellowship with volunteers, health guests, students, and staff. Contact business manager, call **703-672-3100.**

Retirement Living Plans

Still in the planning stages, we would like your input, and a chance to share our ideas with you. Call **703-672-3100.**

Last Generation

A magazine edited and published for young people by Hartland Institute. Subscription rate is $17.95 per year. Contact editor, **703-672-3100.**

Weekend Retreats and Camp Meeting at Hartland

Schedules available upon request. Contact retreat and camp meeting coordinator, **703-672-3100.**

Hartland Institute, P.O. Box 1, Rapidan, Virginia 22733

Last Generation

Last Generation is a monthly magazine specifically focused to the ideals, challenges, and mission of senior high/college-aged young people. Read *Last Generation* from cover to cover each month, and experience the inspirational materials attuned to spiritual life and inner growth. This publication, attractively presented, makes an appropriate gift for many occasions. After you have read the magazine, pass it on or order additional copies for your church, youth clubs, high schools, colleges, or your individual friends.

Special Introductory Offer for *Last Generation*

Check appropriate boxes below.

SEND ME: **Quantity ordered**

❏ 1 year, 12 issues, U.S.A.   US$17.95_____

❏ 1 year, 12 issues, Canada   US$22.95_____

❏ 1 year, 12 issues, Overseas   US$27.95_____

❏ Bulk order (single address)*   QTY Order _____

❏ Payment enclosed $ _____

❏ VISA ❏ MasterCard   Card no. _____ Date of expiration_____

Name_____

Address_____

City_____State _____ ZIP_____

Country _____

Mail to *Last Generation*   VA residents add 4.5% tax.
P.O. Box 1, Rapidan, VA 22733   Prices subject to change without notice:
U.S.A.

Gift Subscription

Check Appropriate boxes below.

SEND ME: **Quantity ordered**

❏ 1 year, 12 issues, U.S.A.   US$17.95_____

❏ 1 year, 12 issues, Canada   US$22.95_____

❏ 1 year, 12 issues, Overseas   US$27.95_____

❏ Payment enclosed $ _____

❏ VISA ❏ MasterCard   Card no. _____ Date of expiration_____

To:

Name_____

Address_____

City_____State _____ ZIP_____

Country _____

From:

Name_____

Address_____

City_____State _____ ZIP_____

Country _____

Mail to *Last Generation*   VA residents add 4.5% tax.
P.O. Box 1, Rapidan, VA 22733   Prices subject to change without notice.
U.S.A.

SPECIAL BULK ORDER PRICES PER ADDRESS:

❏ 2@$15.95ea. ❏ 3@$14.95ea. ❏ 4@$13.95ea. ❏ 5-9@$12.95ea. ❏10-24@$11.95ea.
❏ 24-49@$10.95ea. ❏ 50-99@$9.95ea. ❏100+@$8.95ea.

Other Interesting Books and Videos

Books

Mystical Medicine/Warren Peters **$5.95**

    This book will surprise you with facts on different avenues used to gain healing.

Youth, Do You Dare!/Colin Standish **$4.95**

    New! This book speaks to youth about specific pressures they face—both problems and opportunities—and gives insights to help them strengthen the dimensions of the spiritual values in their lives.

Questions That Demand Answers/Thomas Davis **$6.95**

What Must I Do To Be Saved?, two vol. set/Margret Davis **$17.95**

The Third Angel's Message of Righteousness by Faith/L. Scarbrough   **$5.95**

Inspirational VHS Videos
(approximately four hours each video)

"Education for Today," three videos. Discussion on discipline, entertainment, parenting, competition, and other topics./Dr. Standish **$54.95**

Roundtable on Health with Drs. Peters, Goley, Wilson(2 Tape set) $49.00

.... (single) **$25.00**

Lifestyle to Health Series with Drs. Peters, Wilson, Goley (4 tape set) **$95.00**

On cancer, and other topics **$18.88**

On sugar, disease, and other topics **$18.88**

On exercise, anger, and other topics **$18.88**

On hydrotherapy and other topics **$18.88**

Vegetarian Cookbooks

Hartland Heartsavers, Hartand Staff **$4.95**

Eat for Strength, Regular/A. Thrash **$7.95**

Eat for Strength, Oil Free/A. Thrash **$7.95**

The Joy of Cooking Naturally/P. Dameron **$9.95**

Cooking With Natural Foods/M. Beltz **$14.95**

Weimar Cookbook Country, Life Restaurant **$7.95**

Of These Ye May Freely Eat/J. Rachor **$2.95**

Strict Vegetarian Cookbook/L. Tadej **$7.95**

Something Better/E. Earl & N. Bracket **$8.95**

Nutrition for Vegetarians/A. Thrash **$9.95**

Country Life Cookbook **$10.50**

Prices subject to change without notice.
See reverse side for order form.

Hartland Publications

P.O. Box 1, Rapidan, Virginia 22733

703-672-3566

Order Form

If you are giving a donation or paying for anything other than items on your publication's price list please send a seperate check. Thank you!

Canadian and Foreign customers—checks or money orders must be drawn on U.S. banks in U.S. funds. Prices subject to change without notice.

Name _____

Address _____

City _____ State _____ ZIP _____

Phone _____ Order date _____

Item Description	Quantity	Price	Amount

MasterCard ❏   VISA ❏

Name on card _____

Number on card _____

Expiration date _____

Name of issuing bank _____

SUBTOTAL	
Sales tax (4.5%) VA res.	
Min. postage & handling $1.50	
Orders over $15 + 10% for P/H	
TOTAL DUE	

_____
Customer Signature
X_____
This signature acknowledges this order as correct.

This page intentionally left blank.